A television-radio system is like a nervous system. It sorts and distributes information, igniting memories. It can speed or slow the pulse of society. The impulses it transmits can stir the juices of emotion, and can trigger action. As in the case of a central nervous system, aberrations can deeply disturb the body politic. These complex roles can lend urgency to the study of television and radio and the forces and mechanisms that guide and control them.

—Erik Barnouw, *The Image Empire*

MODELS OF RELIGIOUS
BROADCASTING

by J. Harold Ellens

WILLIAM B. EERDMANS PUBLISHING COMPANY

Copyright © 1974 by William B. Eerdmans Publishing Company
All rights reserved
Printed in the United States of America

Library of Congress Cataloging in Publication Data

Ellens, J   Harold, 1932-
  Models of religious broadcasting.

  Includes bibliographical references.
  1. Radio in religion. 2. Television in religion.
I. Title.
BV656.E43   253.7'8   74-8382
ISBN 0-8028-3437-X
ISBN 0-8028-1506-5 (pbk.)

This book is for Calvin Bulthuis. He conceived the specific idea and encouraged the execution. He died before the book could be finished; but it is really his book, a meager expression of esteem for so gentle, wise, and good a man.

Contents

Preface, 9

One: Technology's Twin, 13
        The Birth of Broadcasting, 13
        Cooperative Religious Efforts, 16
        Denominational Radio, 20
        Television Before 1950, 23

Two: Format Ferment, 26
        The Age of the Orator, 26
        Calls for Renewal, 32

Three: Pulpits and Prophets, 38
        Bishop Sheen, 38
        The Lutheran Hour, 44
        The Back to God Hour, 46
        Charles E. Coughlin, 55

MODELS OF RELIGIOUS BROADCASTING

        Bob Shuler, 61
        Bits and Pieces, 63

Four: Sinai and the Spectacular, 69

        Aimee Semple McPherson, 70
        Rex Humbard, 74
        Oral Roberts, 80
        Billy Graham, 88
        The Divine Invasion, 91

Five: Electronic Education, 95

        Presbyterian Church, US, 97
        United Church of Christ, 100
        The Southern Baptist Convention, 102
        Seventh-Day Adventist Church, 109
        Lutheran Church—Missouri Synod, 114

Six: A Little Leaven, 123

        The United Presbyterian Church, 126
        The Franciscans, 130
        Presbyterian Church, US, 133
        Other Leavening Influences, 135

Seven: The Failed Promise, 140

        Parker's Fight, 140
        Morality in Media, 145
        The Challenge, 147

Bibliography, 153
Index, 165

Preface

Models are short-cuts for communication. They have all the virtues and vices of short-cuts. They can clarify things, but they can as easily obstruct. Nonetheless, communicators of ideas are increasingly resorting to models as means of efficiently expressing complex concepts or processes. Automobiles are modeled to show their qualities for sales purposes. Science classes employ plastic models to teach. Architects prepare three-dimensional models of their building concepts, thus making them more readily appreciated by potential investors.

What is a model? Perhaps it is best defined as a descriptive and symbolic rendering of the essential characteristics of an idea, process, or structure. An architect's model of a building describes its line, form, and proportion, as conceived by its designer. A model of an automobile may symbolically describe the salient characteristics of a specif-

MODELS OF RELIGIOUS BROADCASTING

ic line of autos or it may be one of the line of autos that represents the characteristics of all the others in its line. In any case, models are only representations of reality. They are thus limited. They present only the *salient* features of the real world. They do not describe the whole idea, process, or object they represent.

This book is about models. It is an attempt to describe in symbolic expressions what has been and is happening in the church's use of electronic mass media. There are, we suggest, four basic models in terms of which the history of religious broadcasting can be understood: the pulpit model, the spectacle model, the pedagogical model, and the leaven model. In the chapters that follow we shall describe these models and the way they illuminate what really happens in religious broadcasting. If the church can see more clearly what it is doing and why, it will perceive more readily what it can and ought to do in religious broadcasting.

Models of the real world instruct us. Models of the ideal world can perhaps lift us up to new levels of effectiveness. If so, this book may be redemptive on the first level at least, and prepare for someone wiser than I to inspire us beyond ourselves in employing twentieth-century tools for fulfilling the first-century vision: a universal community of wholesome humans who, because they know the truth, are truly free.

I am indebted to Marion Sharette who typed this manuscript, some of it repeatedly; Mary Jo Ellens, Roland Sharette, and Irene Larson, who read it; Annie Lynch, who read the proofs and prepared the index; and to all the correspondents and interviewees from whom insight and inspiration came. Thanks, friends.

—J. Harold Ellens

MODELS OF RELIGIOUS
BROADCASTING

one
Technology's Twin

The Birth of Broadcasting

Broadcasting is a child of the nineteenth century. The twentieth is its adolescence. This ingenious and unruly child, conceived a hundred years ago, was called to life in a flurry of experiment and intrigue. Vigorous exploration into electronic communication went on all over the western world in the last quarter of the last century. Lonely men in Russia, Germany, France, England, and the Americas passionately stalked the elusive insight or technique that would hurdle the last obstacle to "electric community" and penetrate the last problem.

The breakthrough came with Alexander Graham Bell and the telephone in 1876. From there it was an inevitable thrust to radio: first by wire, then by wireless. Experiments in wireless broadcasting were well along by 1890, thanks to Heinrich Hertz.[1] Popular speculation included television as early as 1879, when George Dumaurier depicted it in *Punch*.[2]

These were great strides in human relations. Already then there were those who saw a major redemptive possibility in a communication system that could transcend geographical separation to bring men together. In effect, space and time were conquered. The only remaining obstacle to unity and mutual affection lay not in man's physical limitations but in the limitations of his spirit. From the outset many believed that broadcasting could become the tool to conquer the "in there" world of man, now that the "out there" was overcome. Utopian visions of paradise regained through electronic mass media were projected before the twentieth century was born. More cautious observers realized at least that a sturdy redemptive potential existed in electronic mass communications.

Broadcasting as we think of it today was born in 1912, when the United States Congress established and President William Howard Taft signed the first radio licensing law. Here was the foundation for the rise and regulation of radio stations across the whole land, frequency assignment by government only, and the development of network broadcasting, with national and international scope. It was a scant six years since the first voice broadcast had been achieved in radio. Reginald Aubrey Fessenden, a Canadian experimenter in code and voice radio, had broadcast a Christmas Eve program to ships at sea in 1906. Quite unexpectedly that night, radio operators off the east coast of the United States heard

> a human voice coming from their instruments—someone speaking! Then a woman's voice rose in song. It was uncanny! Many of them called their officers to come and listen; soon the wireless rooms were crowded. Next someone was heard reading a poem. Then there was a violin solo; then a man made a speech, and they could catch most of the words.[3]

The violin solo (played by Fessenden himself) was Gounod's "O Holy Night." A selection from Luke's Gospel

---

[1] Erik Barnouw, *A Tower in Babel*, Vol. I, p. 9.
[2] *Ibid.*, p. 7.
[3] A. F. Harlow, *Old Wires and New Waves*, p. 455.

had been read. The woman's voice had sung Handel's *Largo*. It is not without significance that that first voice broadcast was a Christian religious celebration. Broadcasting was compelled from the outset to shape itself into the service of human vision, need, and cultural idealism. It was not until considerably later that its primary function became commercial. The growing pains of six decades of broadcasting's adolescence have been apparent. But its adolescence has undeniably shaped American culture.

The 1912 Radio Act required radio operators to be licensed, but did not provide for commercial broadcasting with the complexity that we know today. The Radio Act of 1927 amplified and corrected the old law by imposing careful regulation on the time, place, and quality of broadcasting program, equipment, and frequency use. A system was developed for inspection of broadcasting and licensing of broadcasters. The Radio Act of 1934 established the Federal Communications Commission, basically as it exists today, and laid a detailed foundation for regulating networks and local stations. The 1934 law was amplified by the "Mayflower Doctrine" of 1941. The networks had attempted to hammer out a policy insuring the neutrality of broadcasters in controversial affairs. The FCC Mayflower decision of 1941

> enunciated a somewhat similar doctrine, emphasizing the need for neutrality by licensees. Reprimanding Boston station SAAB for its one-sidedness (but renewing its license) the FCC declared: "A truly free radio cannot be used to advocate the causes of the licensee ... the broadcaster cannot be an advocate."[4]

The increasing complexity of broadcasting law reflected the increasing complexity and aggressiveness of the broadcasting industry.

Already in 1919 Owen D. Young, later to be succeeded by David Sarnoff, founded RCA, an effort, Barnouw calls it, at "an American dominated system of world communication."[5] Broadcasting had already been put into the employ of the nation. On January 8, 1918, President Wilson broadcast his Fourteen Points overseas to the German people, asking them to join a concerned world in the

---

[4]Barnouw, *op. cit.*, Vol. II, p. 137.
[5]*Ibid.*, Vol. I, p. 59.

MODELS OF RELIGIOUS BROADCASTING

pursuit of lasting peace. The broadcast was probably least effective in America, where it did, nonetheless, establish a precedent for presidential use of radio. In 1920 the results that led to Warren Harding's victory in the presidential election were broadcast in Detroit and Pittsburgh. The practice led later to the powerful impact of Franklin D. Roosevelt's "Fireside Chats," John Kennedy's 1962 speech at the Cuban missile crisis, and contemporary campaign television.

In 1901 the *New National Dictionary* was still defining "broadcasting" as the act of planting seeds in a field. It reflected the rural mindset of the nineteenth century. By 1927, "broadcast" was defined as "to disseminate... radio messages." The child was well on its youthful and vigorous way, and the technological age was its twin.

Cooperative Religious Efforts

Religion has been surprisingly prominent in radio broadcasting from the start. At first the predominant form was local religious broadcasts by local churches. Indeed, many churches owned their own stations in those early days.

A month after professional voice broadcasting began in Pittsburgh in December 1920, the Calvary Episcopal Church of that city began to broadcast its worship services. The broadcast medium grew quickly, and within five years there were six hundred radio stations operating in the country, sixty-three of them church-owned.[6] They had been purchased by local congregations as tools for reinforcing and strengthening the image of local ministries.

By the beginning of the 1930s most churches had found it necessary to sell their radio stations to commercial interests because of the onset of the Depression. As that happened, a crucial precedent was set which still controls radio and television—control of program content and production technique by the broadcast industry, not the church. "The use of radio by religious bodies became almost wholly at the discretion of the commercial broad-

---

[6]S. Franklin Mack, "Cooperation in the Use of the Media of Mass Communication." See also W. W. Rodgers, "Broadcasting Church Services," *Radio Broadcast*, Vol. 1 (Aug. 1922), pp. 321ff.

casters in control of stations and network facilities."[7] This control may be exercised directly, as it is when the network or station itself produces the religious programs, or indirectly, as it is by the universal limitation of the types of programs allowed on the air, and the retention by broadcasters of the right to decide who can get reasonably good time slots with what kind of program format and content.

Early in the history of religious broadcasting, there were cooperative and interdenominational efforts as well as local ones. The Federal Council of Churches of Christ (FCCC), which represented at that time twenty-five denominations, encouraged councils of churches in local communities throughout the nation to develop cooperative broadcasting. The idea caught on in most major urban areas. Beginning in 1923, Frank C. Goodman developed three weekly religious programs on New York stations with FCCC encouragement. By 1924 the Greater New York Federation of Churches had begun a weekly broadcast, "National Radio Pulpit," with Dr. S. Parkes Cadman preaching on station WEAF. That station became WNBC in 1926, the NBC network was born, and Cadman's program became network radio.

Once its network operations were well established, NBC turned to the FCCC for cooperation in religious programming. NBC wanted the FCCC to be the sole source of Protestant programming, thus simplifying NBC's task of program control. Moreover, such a cooperative arrangement took care of the problem of having to satisfy numerous denominations with "equal time." The FCCC was delighted with the arrangement, and its general secretary was appointed by NBC to its National Religious Advisory Council. In 1934 the FCCC assumed total responsibility for network Protestant broadcasting and created the department of National Religious Radio. The cooperative arrangement between NBC and the FCCC was permanently to shape the history of religious broadcasting in crucial ways.

[7] Ralph M. Jennings, "Policies and Practices of Selected National Bodies as Related to Broadcasting in the Public Interest, 1920-1950," p. 3.

MODELS OF RELIGIOUS BROADCASTING

The FCCC had six programs on NBC radio. The format of all six was preaching and teaching, with little music, and no drama, news, or children's programming.[8] There were virtues and vices in the NBC-FCCC combine. Broadcasting by local churches, as well as independent and denominational religious broadcasting, felt the influence of practices devised and policies hammered out in New York. The network was increasingly coming to influence local station program schedules. NBC allocated its free public service time exclusively to FCCC programs, leaving its local affiliate stations with a limited amount of public service time for local religious programs. Consequently, many local, denominational, and independent religious broadcasters had no alternative but to purchase time on the air. That precedent still controls religious broadcasting, especially in television. Some relief from the influence of the NBC-FCCC combine was realized when CBS was founded in 1927, the Mutual network in the mid-1930s and ABC in the mid-1940s. The FCCC expanded its operation to use all the networks in a minor way.

Meanwhile the idea of national broadcasting by denominations, independent of both NBC and the FCCC, began to take form, prompted by the desire for more denominational control of program content and more variation in program format. By the mid-1930s many of the denominations supporting the FCCC disliked the absence of innovation and a prophetic dimension in the radio programs being produced. The conviction had arisen that the FCCC broadcasting ministry was in effect imprisoned by the network, and a need for more distinctively Christian broadcasting was felt. The FCCC was accused of being the network's handmaiden, with stronger allegiance to NBC and its free public service programming opportunities than to Christian distinctiveness and creativity.

When the FCCC role as the single major spokesman for Protestant broadcasting fell under siege, significant changes were brought about. The era of unified religious broadcasting ended. Cooperative ventures on a smaller scale were developed among some denominations, but independent

---

[8]William F. Fore, "A Short History of Religious Broadcasting," p. 1.

TECHNOLOGY'S TWIN

broadcasting by all segments of the major faiths became more common.

The most important new cooperative was the Joint Religious Radio Committee (JRRC), organized in 1944 by Everett C. Parker. It included the Congregational, Methodist, Presbyterian USA, Evangelical and Reformed denominations, and the United Church of Canada. Roman Catholic broadcasting at the time was mainly diocesan, with the exception of such independent operations as that of Father Charles E. Coughlin. Jewish broadcasting was inconsequential in the national broadcasting arena. Independent Protestant broadcasting by individuals or denominations outside cooperatives like the JRRC depended mostly on purchased time and on the charisma of the individual broadcaster.

The JRRC proved an imaginative alternate source of religious radio programs. Unlike the FCCC it did not limit its format to preaching and teaching, nor its distribution to one network. As Jennings notes, the JRRC

> demonstrated the value of creatively using the radio medium in religious broadcasting, the potentials of transcribed programs distributed through local religious groups and stations, the need for broadcast education for churchmen using the radio medium, and the necessity for the church to account for the public interest as it related to the entire world of broadcasting.[9]

In addition to its experiments with non-preaching formats and in private syndication (distribution by tape directly to local stations), the JRRC sponsored radio workshops to prepare local pastors for broadcasting and joined NBC to grant fellowships for ministers training in broadcasting.

JRRC influence was so significant that in 1948 the Protestant Radio Commission of the FCCC merged with the JRRC. The new organization maintained the innovation for which the JRRC stood. Dramatic children's programs and numerous missionary education and relief programs for adults were developed. In 1950 the old FCCC became the National Council of Churches of Christ in the USA (NCC). The NCC created a Broadcasting and Film Commission (BFC) to handle all cooperative national Prot-

---

[9]Jennings, *op. cit.*, pp. 220f.

estant broadcasting. Both the NCC and BFC function essentially the same way as under the old FCCC, and the biggest problem of religious broadcasting (especially on the national scale)—being at the mercy of the broadcasting industry—still persists in the 1970s, as we shall see in succeeding chapters.

During the 1940s three additional cooperatives were developed among American Protestants. Both the American Council of Churches (founded in 1941), who claimed to stand for all non-FCCC members, and the National Association of Evangelicals (founded in 1942), who attempted to represent conservative and fundamentalist Christianity, strove for part of the network public service time then dominated by the FCCC. The third group was the Southern Religious Radio Conference (SRRC), organized in Atlanta in 1945. It comprised the national broadcasting ministries of Southern Baptist, Lutheran, Methodist, Presbyterian US, and Protestant Episcopal Churches, although the Southern Baptists withdrew in 1949 in favor of independent denominational broadcasting. The SRRC established a production center in Atlanta in 1953, which functioned until 1968, and whose facilities are still available for broadcast production.

Denominational Radio

By 1944 independent denominational radio with national distribution was fairly common. National distribution for such ventures was independent of FCCC, network, and church cooperatives alike, and used purchased time and station-by-station syndication.

Most American denominations undertook some type of broadcasting ministry at some point in the first half century of radio. A small percentage achieved sustained and successful operations in broadcasting, and nine achieved significant national scope.

The United Presbyterian Church had discussed the prospects of radio ministry as early as 1930. From the outset its main efforts in national radio broadcasting were cooperative with the FCCC. In a review of its broadcasting policy in the mid-1940s, the denomination rejected the idea of independent broadcasting, but did join the JRRC in addition to the FCCC. In 1965 the United Presbyterians began "spot" broadcasting as an independent enterprise with private syndication to local stations.

The Presbyterian Church US began in radio through the SRRC in 1945. In 1963 it undertook independent broadcasting operations. Dr. John Alexander had begun a local radio ministry to military troops in North Carolina in 1944. His leadership resulted in a denominational program called "The Protestant Hour." That program was to become the primary SRRC effort in 1945.

The Southern Baptist Convention established a Radio Committee in 1938, climaxing a long history of local broadcasting by individual congregations and groups of churches.[10] In 1941 the "Southern Baptist Hour" was initiated, using a preaching format on network public service time.[11] For four years, the Baptists were members of the SRRC, until 1949 when all their broadcasting activities were moved to Fort Worth. That move established a permanent pattern of independent broadcasting for the Southern Baptists. The format, both cooperatively and independently, was preaching and teaching with hymns.

In contrast, the national broadcasting ministry of the Protestant Episcopal Church, begun in 1945 when "The Living People" was broadcast for Lent, had an innovative format. A religious situation was dramatized by leading actors, and the program privately syndicated to local stations.[12] The Episcopalians also broadcast "Great Scenes from Great Plays," a series of dramatic radio excerpts from well-known dramas. This was religious programming "without sermons, Bible readings, or hymn singing."[13]

Lutheran efforts at broadcasting began soon. Dr. Walter A. Maier initiated a local broadcast ministry in 1924, and in 1929 "The Lutheran Hour" was initiated as a denominational program of the Lutheran Church—Missouri Synod.

[10]*Annual of the Southern Baptist Convention, 1938*, p. 9; see also p. 63.
[11]*Annual of the Southern Baptist Convention, 1942*.
[12]"Episcopal Church Issues Religious Transcriptions for Use During Lent," *Religious News Service*, January 5, 1945.
[13]Jennings, *op. cit.*, pp. 467ff.

MODELS OF RELIGIOUS BROADCASTING

In 1930 it gained national exposure on the CBS network on purchased time. With its half-hour sermonic format, "The Lutheran Hour" is still the only national radio broadcast of the Missouri Synod Lutherans.[14] The Lutheran Church in America has a national radio ministry with historical roots that go back to 1931 and an early preach-teach format. The enterprise was carried out under the auspices of the FCCC and broadcast over NBC.

The United Methodist Church joined the SRRC in 1946 after some attempts at privately syndicated denominational broadcasting. It remained with the conference until 1963, but continued its private syndications. These included a number of interesting and varied programs during the late forties. Five series of transcriptions were available in 1948:

> "Music For The Soul," eight fifteen-minute programs of devotional music; "The Christians," thirteen dramatizations portraying a Christian family; "So You Want To Stay Married," eight dramatic programs showing strength in Christian families; "Families Need Parents," six dramas on parent-child relationships; and "Holy Week Series," six music and devotional programs.[15]

Established in 1948, the Methodist Radio and Film Commission was first funded in 1952. In the interim the denomination's national broadcasting was handled by the Upper Room Radio Parish and the SRRC. By 1952 there were some six hundred radio stations carrying the programs of Upper Room Radio Parish. The "Family Week" series in 1949 was carried by 1200 stations.

The United Church of Christ has roots in national broadcasting that are interwoven with the ministry of Everett C. Parker. In 1944, when Parker became the prime mover in establishing the JRRC, he was a member of the Congregational Christian Church, and head of the denomination's radio committee. That committee developed and distributed its programs through the JRRC. In 1948, the denominational radio committee was eliminated. Parker moved to head the new Protestant Radio Commission of

---

[14] For the story of "The Lutheran Hour," see Paul L. Maier, *A Man Spoke, A World Listened*, esp. in this connection, pp. 70-72.
[15] Jennings, *op. cit.*, p. 433.

the FCCC. It was not until 1954 that the United Church reestablished a denominational office of communication, headed by Franklin Mack.[16]

With rare exception the radio programming of all these denominations was on free public service time, both in network distribution and private syndication. The JRRC and the SRRC, like the FCCC, employed only free public service time. Most of the denominational work was cooperative, as indicated above. The United Methodists and Episcopalians were the rare exceptions to the general sermonic format in radio, the innovation apparently fostered in both cases by association with the SRRC and/or the JRRC.

Television Before 1950

Television became a serious broadcasting possibility in the United States in 1939. NBC telecast sixty hours of programs and eight hundred hours of test patterns from its New York station in 1939 and 1940 to the estimated three thousand television receivers (with an audience of about fifteen thousand) then in New York.[17] This early experiment included religious programming by the three major faiths. The religious programs were presented in cooperation with the Federal Council of Churches. Jennings observes:

> Noting the event, the Federal Council Bulletin said that its religious telecast was designed for "shut-ins who could not get to services of public worship." While it is not known how many shut-ins may have been among television's then small audience, it seems that the Council was seeking for television a positive service that was non-competitive with traditional worship, an ever-important factor in its rationale for radio broadcasting.[18]

Not until seven years later was further serious consideration given to programming religion for television. The Southern Baptist Convention, by now a large user of radio time in the South and Southwest, considered the matter officially at its annual convention, and decided to move

---

[16]*Ibid.*, pp. 412ff.
[17]Mack, *op. cit.*, p. 7.
[18]Jennings, *op. cit.*, p. 117.

MODELS OF RELIGIOUS BROADCASTING

aggressively into the field. The convention declared: "In a matter of months, Southern Baptists must face the opportunity of this new open door for the propagation of the gospel."[19]

The Missouri Synod Lutherans soon followed, with a vigorous interest in television programming surfacing in the late 1940s. The Synod was petitioned in 1949 for funds for television programming, and Walter A. Maier hailed television as a new medium for preaching. In 1951, however, plans for a televised "Lutheran Hour" were set aside for the development of "This Is the Life," a half-hour dramatic series, which was the first major effort in religious television. During 1949 the FCCC began limited television broadcasting. Everett Parker commented on the church's use of television:

> We have the opportunity to start from scratch in the development of a great new communication art. We must divorce ourselves from all preconceived ideas of conventional methods of the religious message and experiment with various program formats. We must avoid the mistakes of a religious radio which concentrated on one format and diversify our programs.[20]

The first national religious television came in late 1949 through the Protestant Radio Commission of the FCCC. ABC-TV presented a series entitled "I Believe..." on Tuesday evenings, with noted theologians discussing religion as it affected everyday life. The same year a television puppet series began, dramatizing well-known biblical stories—the Good Samaritan, the Prodigal Son, the Lost Sheep, and the Ten Talents.[21]

Network religious television thus had an auspicious beginning. The formats were innovative and suggested exciting future prospects. As the commercial scope and sophistication of television broadcasting grew, so did the ecclesiastical interest in its unusual potentials for religion. From the NBC-FCCC experiment in 1939-1940, and the earnest beginning of network programming in 1949-1950, the

---

[19] *Annual of the Southern Baptist Convention, 1947*, p. 294.
[20] Quoted in: "Parker Named to Key Protestant Post," *Religious News Service*, January 3, 1949.
[21] Jennings, *op. cit.*, pp. 350ff.

TECHNOLOGY'S TWIN

church's involvement and interest in religious television has reflected increasing intensity, variety, and sophistication.

The church's concern in broadcasting is twofold—with its potential as a tool for ministry, and with its potential for shaping social value systems for good or ill. The Federal Council's observations about radio are applicable to television as well:

> The churches have a valid concern... quite apart from... specifically religious use. Nothing that affects the social wellbeing can fail to be of concern to organized religion. In particular, the fact that broadcasting enters so largely into home life makes it incumbent upon the Christian Church to maintain an intelligent and active interest in its future development. The churches have no more right than other institutions to dictate the policies of the industry, but they have a definite obligation to make their influence felt and to co-operate with the industry in the progressive improvement of its standards.[22]

This latter concern has been pointedly expressed in semi-theological terms by the United Presbyterian Church USA.

> Why should the church be concerned with broadcasting? This is the basic question and here are some of the basic answers: because there is a Great Commission—"Go into all the world and preach the Gospel..."; because the majority of the mass audience only nods toward the church, politely or negatively, when it appears on radio or television;... because the church *must* involve itself in the techniques, problems and opportunities of mass communication if it is to fulfill the Great Commission.[23]

That has been the church's propelling motivation in television; and so, a major aspect of her concern in broadcasting has been for genuinely effective program formats. As in the history of religious radio, so in the history of religious television strong voices have continually called for the church to use maximum creativity in programming technique and to keep pace with the techniques of the industry.

---

[22]Department of Research and Education of the Federal Council of Churches of Christ, *Broadcasting and the Public*, p. 7.
[23]*A Communications Manual for Judicatories of the Church*, Part I: "Broadcasting," p. 1.

two
Format Ferment

The Age of the Orator

Anyone with a product to sell is well aware of the importance of packaging. The same applies when one is promoting the good news of the Christian gospel. The package may attract, or detract, or distract. Consequently, from the start of religious broadcasting, churchmen and broadcasters alike have been concerned about its packaging. Ferment over the format of religious radio and television has continued for half a century.

When religious broadcasting began in the 1920s, it seemed natural to proclaim the word of God on radio by preaching. The age was an auspicious one for rhetoric. Americans still celebrated the heroic orator. Remnants of the nineteenth century like William Jennings Bryan were stalking the Chautauqua circuit. Pulpit rhetoric was virtually the only form of proclamation employed by the church. A "worship service" was a preaching service—and the great preachers held forth in long sermons full of color, clarity, and, usually, Christian dogmatism. Thus when the microphone began to carry man's voice to the masses and the world became the parish, religious leaders naturally saw radio as an enlarged pulpit. They contracted it for preaching religion.

In establishing the "National Radio Pulpit" in 1924 Frank Goodman apparently gave no consideration to any broadcasting format except the sermon. Reflecting the mindset of the age, he built the series around heroic orators. S. Parkes Cadman, Harry Emerson Fosdick, Ralph Sockman, and David H. C. Read represent the tradition established for and by "National Radio Pulpit." The tradition has had a not inconsiderable influence on religious broadcasting format since.

Nevertheless, there have always been voices raised against this predominance of the "pulpit." As broadcasting techniques in the infant industry developed, the broadcasters themselves called on the church for greater innovation in format. A more startling and entertaining type of program was necessary to hold larger "uncommitted" audiences. Already in 1923 a clear stand was registered in favor of varied and innovative formats for religious broadcasting.

> It becomes apparent that we have not to consider the question, shall radio be utilized for broadcasting religion, but rather should radio be used by this particular church for broadcasting the particular form of worship used by this church?[1]

The FCCC joined the struggle over program format in 1924. It urged the programming of "not only services of worship but also addresses on the church's interest in some of the great social and international issues of the day."[2] This, however, signaled no departure from pulpit rhetoric; it only marked a change in subject matter. Religious broadcasting format simply did not keep pace with the industry.

---

[1] "Some Problems in the Broadcasting of Religion," *Radio Broadcast*, Vol. IV (Nov. 1923), p. 11.
[2] "Radio in the Churches," *Federal Council Bulletin*, Vol. VII (Nov./Dec. 1924), p. 6.

MODELS OF RELIGIOUS BROADCASTING

The National Broadcasting Company insisted that only studio programs designed for the radio, and not ordinary church services, should go on the air under its auspices.... It is not, however, the dominating sentiment of church groups throughout the country. There is a widespread feeling that religious radio services should consist in broadcasting nothing but an actual church service.[3]

In 1928, NBC invited the FCCC General Secretary, Dr. Charles S. MacFarland, to join the network's new Religious Advisory Council in an effort to bring the religious broadcasters into harmony with the network. MacFarland and his Catholic and Jewish counterparts on the Council, Morgan J. O'Brien and Julius Rosenwald, arrived at a statement of principles:

1. Religious groups should receive free time, but *pay* for their production costs.
2. Religious broadcasting should be non-denominational.
3. It should use one man as the program "star" for continuity.
4. It should use a preaching format.
5. It should avoid matters of doctrine and controversial subjects.[4]

This policy statement subsequently became the foundation on which the FCCC built its entire broadcasting operation and policy, the controlling influence in all cooperative Protestant broadcasting until Everett Parker created the JRRC in reaction against the limitation of format to preaching, and the "personality" cult implied in the "use of one man for continuity." Moreover, it was only in the late 1960s that genuinely creative efforts at innovative format became prominent in religious broadcasting, and most of these were limited to television.

Custom was not the sole factor leading the church to a preaching format. From the early days of religious radio the factor of funding influenced program packaging. Funding problems are related to the broadcasting industry's policy on allocation and cost of air time. Since the 1930s,

[3]"Preaching to a Nation," *Review of Reviews*, Vol. LXXIX (Feb. 1929), p. 134.
[4]Fore, "A Short History of Religious Broadcasting," p. 1.

FORMAT FERMENT

when most churches sold their broadcasting stations to commercial interests, the church has had only two ways to gain air time: to acquire free time from local or network broadcasters, or to buy time from the broadcasters. When free time is offered it is a public service, and the religious broadcaster is at the mercy of the industry as to how long and when his broadcast will air. It is safe to assume that it will not be prime audience time. To purchase air time, on the other hand, is to compete with wealthy commercial institutions for prime audience time, and religious groups have often had difficulty paying the price for that.

When "air time" is a funding problem, program production suffers. Such religious broadcasters as the late Charles E. Fuller, Aimee Semple McPherson, Charles E. Coughlin, M. R. De Haan, Fulton Sheen, and Peter Eldersveld put most of their funds into buying air time. That left minimal funds for program production. Since the preaching format is the least costly, the money problem reinforced the tendency to see pulpit rhetoric as the best use of broadcast resources.

Over the years, the Federal Radio Commission (later the Federal Communications Commission or FCC) developed its policy regarding the availability of air time for various kinds of community organizations. Under this policy broadcasters at the local and network level are required to provide free air time at regular intervals for broadcasting programs that are "in the public interest." By 1929 the Commission had ruled that religious broadcasting was a necessary program category for broadcasting in the "public interest, convenience, and necessity."[5]

In 1940 NBC reorganized its operations and placed an educator, James Roland Angell, in charge of all of what came to be called "public service programming." The broadcasters' opinion of religious programming was stated by the National Association of Broadcasters:

> To every American, the Bill of Rights guarantees the privilege to worship as conscience dictates, without fear of intimidation or reprisal. Radio, therefore, which reaches men of all creeds and

[5]United States Federal Communications Commission, "Public Service Responsibility of Broadcast Licensees," pp. 10, 13.

MODELS OF RELIGIOUS BROADCASTING

races simultaneously, may not be used to convey attacks upon another's race or religion. Rather it should be the purpose of the religious broadcaster to promote the spiritual harmony and understanding of mankind, to administer to the religious needs of the community and to contribute to the spiritual nourishment and uplift of the individual.[6]

It was no doubt this assertion (made in 1939) that broadcasters have a responsibility to avoid sectarianism and to promote actively the pursuit of religious objectives, which influenced NBC to move toward more effective use of public service time for religious purposes.

Neither the FCCC nor the denominations understood or agreed with this concept of the industry's responsibility. In consequence, religious broadcasters defeated their own purposes. By failing to see religious broadcasting as the industry's community responsibility and instead looking on it as a gift from the industry, they placed religious broadcasting on an unstable foundation. This posture led eventually to the accusation that the FCCC felt obligated to NBC and that such allegiance compromised both the integrity of the Council and its responsibility for creative programming.[6a] The FCCC was certainly not afraid to use its unique relationship with NBC as a lever to control network religion as well as denominational broadcasting. Throughout the 1930s and 1940s the FCCC maintained a policy of *requesting* time for itself alone as the major representative of religion in broadcasting.[7]

Thus the largest and most influential national agency of religious broadcasting was making no effort to compel the industry to see religious broadcasting costs in air time and program production as an industry responsibility to the community. In other words, the FCC (the government) was improving conditions for creative religious broadcasting, at the same time that the FCCC (the church) was obstructing that development.

The 1941 decision of the FCC to forbid networks from

---

[6]"Stringent Code Is Submitted to Industry," *Broadcasting*, Vol. XVI (June 15, 1939), p. 9.

[6a]Jennings, "Policies and Practices of Selected National Bodies," pp. 482-92.

[7]Fore, *op. cit.*, p. 3.

FORMAT FERMENT

executing contracts that bound affiliated stations to exclusive network programming was an important one for religious broadcasting,[8] since this encouraged local programming, denominational programming outside the FCCC, and private syndication by independent or cooperative agencies.

But the confrontation of the broadcasting industry with its community responsibility to fund prime air time as well as production costs of religious programs did not surface again until the late 1960s. The industry's policies and practices are interesting and significant. From its inception as a national network in 1926 NBC provided free time for religious broadcasting through the FCCC and its successors. From 1927, when it was established, CBS sold time for religious broadcasting. It continued that policy and practice until 1931, when it moved toward public service programming. The Mutual Broadcasting System, established in the mid-1930s, made only purchased time available for religious broadcasting. It secured contracts from denominational sources. The purchased time was initially provided in one-hour segments. In the mid-1940s, about the time of the rise of the JRRC, purchased time was limited to half-hour segments and some public service time was provided to religious broadcasters. All religious programming on ABC, established in the mid-1940s, was free public service time until 1949 when it began to sell time for religious programming.[9]

The rationale behind the NBC policy was that selling time might result in disproportionate influence by the individuals or groups with the most money. Like NBC, ABC provided time to each of the three major faiths rather than try to serve every denomination or offshoot who wanted to buy time. CBS built its own religious program, consisting of two half-hour Sunday worship programs, one in the early morning, one in the late evening. Mutual limited commercial religious programs to a half hour each on Sunday morning, and forbade direct solicitation of

---

[8]United States Federal Communications Commission, *Report on Chain Broadcasting.*
[9]Jennings, *op. cit.*, pp. 482-92.

MODELS OF RELIGIOUS BROADCASTING

funds over the air. Although the National Association of Evangelicals accused the FCCC of forcing paid religious broadcasting off the air, a number of conservative Protestant radio ministries thrived due to audience support of their follow-up materials.[10]

Calls for Renewal

The most serious defect of the still-prevalent preaching format was stated by Everett C. Parker at the founding of the JRRC in 1944: "Present-day religious broadcasting is not listened to by the great bulk of the population."

> It is not sufficient to transpose a sermon from the pulpit to the microphone. The new medium requires a new approach. We plan to employ professional script writers, actors, musicians, and directors to bring into the American homes the religious message with all the forcefulness and appeal contained in leading sponsored programs. We do not conceive this to mean any "watering down" of religion's appeal by radio. Rather, by heightening the dramatic appeal of the program, we intend to increase its impact and add to its audience.[11]

The theological journals became heralds of the need for renewal in religious broadcasting format. Reflecting on why religious broadcasting was so dull and unappealing, *The Chicago Theological Seminary Register* concluded that it was

> (a) because religious broadcasters have not taken advantage on a large scale of more than one or two of the many successful program techniques which have been devised for radio; (b) because religious programs are seldom beamed at specific listener groups (i.e., women, children, youth, etc.) but attempt to reach all classes of people at all times; (c) because large numbers of religious broadcasters are not trained in the writing, producing, and performing of radio programs; (d) because local religious groups often fail to service their sustaining time with adequate promotion and program preparation; (e) because the content of religious programs often is not suited to the needs of the average listener.[12]

[10]Fore, *op. cit.*, p. 3.
[11]Everett C. Parker as quoted in "Protestant Groups Form Radio Committee," *Religious News Service*, January 2, 1945. A similar sentiment had been expressed by Fred Eastman, "Religion and the Radio," *The Christian Century*, Vol. LVIII (Mar. 6, 1941), p. 349.
[12]"Big Business in Religious Radio," *The Chicago Theological Seminary Register*, Vol. XXXIV (Mar. 1944), p. 22.

FORMAT FERMENT

Christian Century took up the cry as well.

> In spite of the fact that radio affords the most powerful medium of mass influence in history, with opportunities to reach a vast, heterogeneous audience, untouched by conventional church activities, its use by religious leaders has been lamentable, unintelligent and ineffective. The typical preaching and devotional type of programs have a rightful place on networks and local station schedules but they need much improvement and they need to be supplemented by other types of religious broadcasts. Regardless of how popular the preacher may be these programs often lack the common touch, the dramatic, mass appeal which is the genius of radio.... They must be good radio, using all the successful techniques of professional production.[13]

As the presence of the JRRC began to be felt in industry and church, some new programming series were attempted by the FCCC over NBC, CBS, and Mutual. Unfortunately, they tended to fall into traditional preach-teach formats, but in fifteen-minute rather than half-hour segments. From 1945 to 1948 public service time was made available to the FCCC, NAE, American Council of Churches of Christ, the National Council of Catholic Men, and the like.[14]

The first JRRC series was aired in 1945—"The Radio Edition of the Bible," which used Old and New Testament passages as the basis for dramatic sketches, produced by Erik Barnouw and played by name actors and actresses. The second series was the children's program "All Aboard for Adventure"; the third came in 1947 with fifteen documentaries entitled, "To You in America." The "Building for Peace" series followed in 1948. All of these series were privately syndicated over as many as 500 stations.[15] The FCCC started to take notice:

> The churches have not found ways fully to use the modern means of communication for the spread of the Christian Gospel. The unchurched of America cannot be reached in any adequate way unless the church uses media which mold men's convictions—motion pictures—radio—television—drama—the press—popular literature—and the whole field of organized advertising. A good question for the church to ask is, "Must the church abdicate from these powerful means of propaganda, and relinquish them, with their all-pervasive influence, to the forces of secularism?"

[13] Charles M. Crowe, "Religion on the Air," *Christian Century*, Vol. LX (Aug. 23, 1944), p. 974.
[14] Jennings, *op. cit.*, p. 185.
[15] *Ibid.*, pp. 213ff.

MODELS OF RELIGIOUS BROADCASTING

> Of all the modern agencies of propaganda only broadcasting has been at all adequately used by the church. Today, religious broadcasting is the great modern power for indirect evangelism offered to the church. *New and better ways must be found for the presentation of the Christian message to the unchurched of the nation through radio.*[16]

One suspects that this conversion of the FCCC came too late. An apparently irreversible pattern regarding religious broadcasting had become ingrained in the industry: religious programming was simply relegated to "ghetto" time—that time during the broadcast day or week when the desired audience is least likely to be available. Today, religious programs are falling deeper and deeper into ghetto time on both radio and television, except for "short segment" religious programs, which are inserted into cartoon series on prime children's time, or presented occasionally as ten- to sixty-second commercials in prime time.

The reason for airing religion in ghetto time is clear: money. If the industry is seen as doing the religious broadcaster a favor in the first place the pattern will persist. If, however, the broadcaster is forced to see religious broadcasting as a public service responsibility, as the FCC insists, perhaps the pattern can be broken. Parker believes it can and must be.

In any case, broadcasting industry policy and limitation of money and vision in the church have held religious broadcasting to a role in society that is hardly worthy of the enormous potential of the broadcast media. Reacting some years ago to the televised coverage of Eisenhower's funeral and noting its evidence of TV's seldom realized potential to reach the spirit of men, *New York Times* columnist James Reston was in effect issuing a challenge to the church. Ronn Spargur pointed to the difficulty of meeting Reston's challenge:

> For the most part, churches are not inclined to give up the principle that programs should follow Sunday-service formats. They have produced few contemporary programs able to entertain and to tempt the viewer's spiritual appetite at the same time. The churches are still trying to reach people within the confines of formal worship, and not on the level where they live.

[16]*Biennial Report, 1946*, pp. 105,149.

FORMAT FERMENT

Here is an obvious impasse. Television is not going to make any time concessions until religious programming shows that it can compete. And religious programming is not going to compete until talented people are convinced that what they created is not going to be buried in the Sunday-morning ghetto.[17]

The same point could be made for radio. Everett Parker thinks the problem is even deeper than funds, timing, and imagination. He feels that religious broadcasters do not understand what the church wants to or ought to achieve in broadcasting.

> If religion on television is to undertake an interpretive role, great sophistication in our handling of the medium will be needed. We are working in an environment where manipulation of people is practiced as a matter of course and as a matter of policy in behalf of the purposes of the sponsor. Some of the most successful television techniques are those designed for the calculated motivation of audiences for purposes that all too seldom are made explicit to them. Without subscribing to the mass communication psychology of manipulation, religious groups may find themselves practicing it unwittingly, compromising their fundamental principles when they believe they are only adapting professional communication techniques to the service of the gospel. . . .
>
> Religious organizations make extensive use of television, radio, movies, and the mass circulation press. Yet the churches never have been able to determine the role to be assigned to these media in the implementation of policy. Exactly what functions do the churches expect television, radio, motion pictures, and the press to perform? This question goes largely unanswered, both nationally and locally. Indeed, it is a question that Protestant policy makers, at least, seem never to have taken seriously.[18]

William Kuhns lays the blame for that at the feet of the theologians, who have yet to develop an adequate theology of communication.

> Though the churches have reluctantly admitted the presence and vaguely conceived power of the new media, their response has been shaped almost entirely by their own ecclesiological mindframe. The media now draw people with the magnetic strength the churches once held, yet the churches' only tactic in face of this situation—with television especially operative as the center of our society's communications—is to "counter" *Bonanza* with

---

[17]Ronn Spargur, "Can Churches Break the Prime-Time Barrier?", *Christianity Today*, Vol. XIV (Jan. 16, 1970), p. 3.
[18]Everett C. Parker, *Religious Television*, pp. ix, 13, 17.

MODELS OF RELIGIOUS BROADCASTING

Lamp Unto My Feet. As the image of man projected in commercials and TV shows moves radically further from the traditional Christian conception of man, priests, ministers, and religious educators search helplessly for those rare original films that express Christian values in a relevant way. Theologically the problem is just as critical: theologians seem to have agreed that the revolution in media in no way presents any real significance for the content and expression of theology today.[19]

It must be noted, in fairness, that the format ferment in religious broadcasting is marked by some concerted efforts at both justifying the traditional patterns and varying them. Some religious broadcasters, like Joel Nederhood of "The Back to God Hour" (Christian Reformed), defend the preaching format on the ground that preaching is the proper technique for the "authoritative apostolic proclamation of the Word of God." Despite recent minor efforts to vary the length of its programs by using short inserts of five to ten minutes and some minute spots, the twenty-five-minute sermonic program still dominates "The Back to God Hour" ministry. Even the shorter segments are sermonic in design. The net result tends to be the attraction of a church-oriented audience tuned in to the sermonic communication of religion. The broadcast spends well over a million dollars annually, nearly all of it for purchased time. The production budget is relatively insignificant.

By contrast, Paul Stevens of the Southern Baptist Convention devotes most of his annual budget of two million dollars to production. The variety of his program format, including documentary, interview, dialogue, "spots," and cartoons is so creative that he can acquire free time across the nation, including network prime time.

From the early 1930s until the rise of television, the preaching format prevailed in religious broadcasting. Interview, dialogue, and drama were seldom heard. The sermonic format moved directly into television during the early fifties but the work done by Parker's JRRC brought some change. The National Council of Churches attempted to get into television with the preaching pattern, but an immediate demand was raised for a more sophisticated use of both audio and video potentials for more attractive and

[19]William Kuhns, *The Electronic Gospel*, p. 16.

FORMAT FERMENT

dramatic programs. Particularly since then, the ferment over format in religious broadcasting has been vigorous. The continuing struggle is to find ways to employ the amazing media of broadcasting for the fulfilment of the Great Commission. Not surprisingly, different people have different ideas about how that should be done. The result is differing practices and rationales among religious broadcasters. These differences can be subsumed under four basic format categories. Some religious broadcasters use the camera and microphone as an extended pulpit; others as tools to create a spectacle; still others to teach, and, finally, others merely to provoke earnest thought.

With a careful analysis of these four techniques or models of religious broadcasting, it may be possible for the church and other religious groups or organizations to see more clearly what should be done in the future. Since the church's main business is communication, the profound potentials of contemporary media must be employed with maximum efficiency and effect. The following chapters, therefore, consider separately what we have called—for convenience' sake—Pulpit, Spectacle, Pedagogy, and Leaven. A chapter on Everett C. Parker's current posture of dissent from all those techniques concludes the discussion and faces the church toward the long future.

three

Pulpits and Prophets

Bishop Sheen

Fulton John Sheen is surely one of the most memorable of all religious broadcasters. Among sophisticated intellectuals and common men alike, it is Bishop Sheen of those who have made radio and television speak for God, who is most remembered and most admired. His broadcasts are a legend a decade and a half after their termination.

Two things made Sheen a flamboyant success in radio and television—his enormous self-confidence and the superlative style with which he expressed it on his broadcasts. There was in him enough of the Old Testament prophet, the prima donna, and modern Madison Avenue to make him a star. For Sheen's prime broadcasting years were the age of the personality cult. He flourished in radio at the time of Edward R. Murrow and Gabriel Heater; he came to television with Ed Sullivan and Bob Hope. After five years of glorious effect in television Sheen gave it up. When he attempted a return in 1959, he could not catch the same fire again. He had not changed, but the audience had moved beyond the flamboyant star-cult of the fifties. Broadcasting was moving into the "confrontation" formats of the sixties. The poetry and rhetoric were giving way to a new kind of "realism."

Sheen was born on May 8, 1895, in a farming and shopkeeping family in El Paso, Illinois. Baptized "Peter John," he felt the name had the wrong ring for him and insisted on "Fulton," after his maternal family. He was educated in St. Paul's Seminary and ordained in 1919. Graduate study at Catholic University of America, the University of Louvain in Belgium, and in Rome demonstrated his agile and profound intellectual prowess. He was awarded a Ph.D. in 1923 and a D.D. a year later.

Most of Sheen's active ministry was in University teaching—a year in dogmatics at St. Edmunds in England and then twenty-five years at Catholic University of America. He spent an interim year of "obedience" in a Peoria parish, but his heart and mind lay in the world represented by the chair of Philosophy of Religion at Catholic University. In 1934 he was appointed Papal Chamberlain, in 1935 Domestic Prelate, in 1950 National Director of the Society for the Propagation of the Faith. On June 11, 1951, he became a bishop, an office he held for eighteen years. Many felt he should have been a Cardinal, perhaps even Pope.

But the popularity of the prolific Bishop (he published over seventy notable books, as well as innumerable newspaper columns), one of the most sought-after preachers and lecturers in the nation, did not extend to his fellow clergy. The bishop who assigned him the year of "obedience" in a humble parish after his return from Europe saw a "wanton arrogance" in him.[1] Though he was famous on the Catholic University campus, his academic load was small—only one graduate course a year for much of his

---

[1] D. P. Noonan, *The Passion of Fulton Sheen*, p. 16.

MODELS OF RELIGIOUS BROADCASTING

career. But his method of teaching was to lecture, not to solicit discussions. His superior once urged him to engage in more dialogue with the students, to which his answer was, "My explanations are so clear there could not possibly be any questions."[2]

Much of Sheen's career featured a strong rivalry with Cardinal Spellman of New York. When Sheen was brought to New York in 1951 to head the Society for the Propagation of the Faith, it was the Cardinal, then a prime mover in papal affairs, who elevated him. As a young priest in Rome Spellman had made the right friends. Now in his powerful position in the Archdiocese of New York he could use those contacts in Rome with real influence.

Sheen's effectiveness as head of the Society for the Propagation of the Faith was quickly evident. He raised millions of dollars in America for overseas missions. He established many new foreign missions. His fame in the church and the world grew rapidly. He was on urgent demand for addresses and broadcasts everywhere in the nation. All these strengths soon made him a threat to Spellman.

The rivalry occasionally flared into outright conflict. On one occasion Pope Pius XII called both men to Rome to settle an altercation that developed when Spellman tried to bill the Society for the Propagation of the Faith for surplus food he had collected from the U. S. Government for the "needy overseas." When Sheen learned that Spellman had received the goods *gratis* he refused to pay. Spellman was badly embarrassed by the incident and, according to Noonan, vowed to get even.

Added to Sheen's intransigence was his great success in the public eye. He had preached on the first program of "The Catholic Hour" in 1930, when a dedicated group of Catholic laymen undertook to promote religious radio. He had gone on to become perhaps the best-known Catholic apologist in Protestant America. In 1952 he switched from his huge success in radio to television, his most successful role.

---

[2]*Ibid.*, p. 19.

All this was too much for Spellman. In 1957 the Cardinal moved to take Sheen out of broadcasting, away from his beloved audience and public acclaim. Sheen had given the Lenten sermons each year for many years at Spellman's church, St. Patrick's Cathedral. Now the Cardinal stopped inviting Sheen and, according to Noonan, forbade his parish priests to do so.[3] In 1966 Sheen went to Rochester as a bishop. The diocese remembered him as a photogenic and charismatic television personality, a worldwide hero of the faith. But Sheen's tenure in Rochester was undistinguished. Not knowing his constituency, he made some unwise choices of causes to support and ended up discrediting himself—not for lack of style or courage, but for lack of common sense. In 1969 he resigned and retired.

Sheen's success as a broadcaster was no accident. His style was carefully orchestrated. He never used notes, since to do so would destroy the spontaneous sincerity he wanted to convey. What suitor, he wondered, uses notes when he proposes marriage?[4] He fretted about and resisted the demands that he supply a written text ahead of time for the broadcasters.

Nevertheless, Sheen spent perhaps thirty hours preparing for each thirty-minute program. Preparation began five to six days before the program, with notes on yellow pads, augmented by ideas for jokes from his associates. He formulated his opening and closing statements concisely; the intervening time developed the subject—always from memory. His thought content was philosophical and humanistic, "a mixture of common sense, logic, and Christian ethics."[5]

Sheen usually delivered his message in Italian or French in a local convent before broadcasting it. When he finally came on camera it was hard to predict what would happen. "At one moment he was humorous. Another moment he would write on the blackboard. Then he would stride toward the cameras, eyes blazing, declaiming as a twen-

---
[3]*Ibid.*, p. 80.
[4]*Ibid.*, p. 52.
[5]*Ibid.*, p. 56.

tieth-century Savanarola."⁶ The discourse continued to the last few seconds of the program. When the broadcasters wanted to close "Life Is Worth Living" with a short musical insert, Sheen resisted. His sense of timing was masterful. Like an experienced actor, he knew "when to move upstage, when to modulate his voice, when to 'throw away' a line, when to ease tension with one of his studiously corny jokes."⁷ Sheen himself once said, "In television, one must always time himself from the end, not the beginning. Decide how many minutes one needs for conclusion. Suppose it's three minutes. Then just three minutes before the appointed time, swinging gracefully from the body of the talk to the conclusion, one finishes right on the nose."⁸ On television he exploited to the full his striking visual impact: the tall, lean figure, his dark, penetrating eyes (underlit to highlight their effect), and his striking black cassock with red cape.

The magnitude of Sheen's ego and the magnificence of his style may have brought him conflict in ecclesiastical circles, but they served him well on stage. A rhetoric text from an earlier day suggests some elements of effective speaking:

> A man speaking is four things, all of them needed in revealing his mind to others. First he is a will, an intent, a meaning which he wishes others to have, a thought. Second, he is a user of language, molding thought and feeling into words. Third, he is a thing to be heard, carrying his purpose, and words to others, through voice. Last, he is a thing to be seen, shown to the sight, a being of action to be noted, and read through the eye.⁹

If these are the essential stuff of good television preaching, Sheen's success is not hard to explain. He mastered the disciplines of thought, language, voice, and bodily action to the point of near perfection. This skill and discipline was the product of vigorous and persistent hard work over many years.

> Sheen was gifted by God with a potentially superior mind, which long years of study hones to a sharp edge. The resonant voice, the

---

⁶*Ibid.*, p. 56.
⁷Van Horne, *Theatre Arts*, Dec. 1952, p. 65.
⁸F. J. Sheen, *Life Is Worth Living*, pp. 194-99.
⁹Charles M. Woolbert, *The Fundamentals of Speech*, p. 3.

limpid power of expression, the dramatic gesture for which he later became famous—these were the result of dedicated effort and discouraging year after year practice.[10]

Sheen was as sensitive as Cicero to the value of believability, as concerned as Aristotle for persuasion by ethical, emotional, and logical proof of the truth of one's convictions. So he argued his case with the vigor and precision of a university philosophy professor. He illustrated his message with the sentiment and even sentimentality that fit his audience. He informed his audience, but he also excited and reassured them.

Despite some objections, his being a bishop appearing in so surprising a setting helps explain his credibility—at least among Catholics. But Roger Ailes, a broadcasting specialist, contends that Sheen's credibility to an interdenominational audience that included many Protestants and Jews was deeper than status—or style, drama, ego, and discipline—would explain. People believed Sheen because of his absolute confidence in what he was saying and doing. He worked overtime to insure that his effective technique of thought and expression conveyed precisely that sense of conviction.

Sheen's selection of topics helped. He dealt with the issues most people were concerned about and regarding which they developed strong feelings. Rather than Catholic doctrine or sectarian apologetics, Sheen's speeches in the 1950s concentrated on Communism and Stalin, God's love, man's soul, the quest for peace, the aimlessness of modern life. He saw himself as a thoughtful and persuasive conversationalist with America, not as a Catholic cleric announcing truth. His role was that of one who offered possible solutions to vexing human problems. He supported this pursuit with an analytical bent of mind and a prodigious volume of reading in many fields. His fine sense of drama put it all together.

When the audience was still tuned to preaching, when classical rhetoric was still in the back of the mind in our culture, Sheen read his audience accurately. His person and

---

[10]William J. Hanford, "Rhetorical Study of the Radio and Television Speaking of Bishop Fulton John Sheen," p. 108.

MODELS OF RELIGIOUS BROADCASTING

style worked well on the television of the fifties. But by the end of his great decade that cultural posture had gone and Sheen could not recapture his lost glory. Some thought his return to television in 1959 would be a spectacular second coming, but it fizzled.

The Lutheran Hour

No denomination has been about the business of radio preaching longer than the Lutheran Church—Missouri Synod. Already in 1924 one of its most notable pastors was preaching over the radio. Dr. Walter A. Maier, styled by *Time* in 1943 as the "Chrysostom of American Lutheranism," was as effective before a microphone as in the pulpit. He began his broadcast from an attic in St. Louis to a few nearby radio receivers. In 1930 his program went on the CBS network and became "The Lutheran Hour." Eventually, more than twelve hundred stations carried his messages to twenty million people. Today, nearly every community in the USA and many nations around the world can hear Oswald C. J. Hoffmann carry on in the tradition of the program's founder.

Maier's pioneering efforts eventually went out in thirty-six languages. When he died in 1950, more people had heard him preach than any other person in history. "The notables of the nation called him, 'the pre-eminent voice of Protestant faith and practice,' 'one of Christendom's greatest leaders,' 'most influential clergyman of all time,' and responsible for a 'world-wide spiritual crusade.' "[11]

CBS, however, had terminated Maier's program within three years of its beginning due to uncertain finances and the policy of the network to limit religious broadcasting to Sunday morning.[12] Maier's ministry during those thirty-six months, however, had been such a stimulating address to the intellect, will, and emotions of the radio audience that "The Lutheran Hour" had to return. A group of Detroit pastors invited Maier to a Detroit radio ministry in 1935. WXYZ carried "The Lutheran Hour of Faith and

---

[11] Paul L. Maier, *A Man Spoke, A World Listened*, p. 2.
[12] "Lutheran Layman's League Bulletin," No. 7.

Fellowship" each Sunday afternoon. WLW of Cincinnati soon added its powerful voice to the ministry. Soon the entire Mutual Network, with which WXYZ and WLW were affiliated, was airing Maier; and "The Lutheran Hour" had returned to its national ministry. Detroit automaker Walther S. Knudsen underwrote the cost. Brace Beemer, "the Lone Ranger," coached Maier in radio rhetoric, only to hear him go his own indomitable way. The ministry grew dramatically. There were sixty thousand letters in response to the program in 1936, ninety thousand in 1937, a hundred twenty-five thousand in 1938.

Network broadcasting is still important to "The Lutheran Hour," although network radio is not as influential as it once was. Consequently, the program is also heard on many independent stations today.

"The Lutheran Hour" has always been, unapologetically, preaching. When Maier preached, he *was* the program. When Hoffmann preaches, he *is* the program. The length of the program may vary—Hoffmann uses thirty-, fifteen-, and two-minute programs—but preaching is the constant. There is a musical introduction and closing, but it is merely setting and staging, not message. The style of Hoffmann, like Maier before him, has been the style of authority, conveyed by voice, personality, and unequivocating content. He insists:

> I speak an authoritative Word. I feel I am speaking *for Christ. His* message has a theological base. That is why there is a sense of authority inevitably present and implied. I am a preacher and a missionary. My mandate and program is the word spoken as Christ's Word without equivocation and with affirmation of the unquestioned content of the Scripture's message.
>
> I simply tell the good news of Jesus Christ. I home in on the cross in every program. I try to find and to start people where they are and help them seriously ask the question, "What does the Lord Jesus expect of me?"[13]

"The Lutheran Hour" currently reaches 125 countries with broadcasts in forty foreign languages. Its estimated weekly audience is forty million. Among its largest ministries are those in Japan, Korea, Mozambique, Nigeria, and

---

[13] Personal interview with the author.

the Philippines. Production centers are located in St. Louis and many foreign cities. Though the high saturation broadcast areas for "The Lutheran Hour" in the United States tend to be parts of the country with a concentration of Lutheran churches, it is clear from the massive foreign ministry that this radio work is not just an electronic reinforcement of denominational loyalty, but mission in the classic sense. "We promote the gospel first and foremost," Hoffmann says, "not the church." The large follow-up program of the broadcast is handled by the church, not by the broadcasting agency. Hoffmann is insistent that his "business is broadcasting. We are not running the church's mission for it."

In all of these ministries the only exception to the preaching format was in the Orient. In Japan, where "The Lutheran Hour" began broadcasting in 1951, drama was the only medium for the first twenty years. It was a striking success. By its tenth anniversary the Japan "Lutheran Hour" was carried to ten million listeners by ninety stations. By its twentieth anniversary a million audience letters had been received, and three-quarters of a million Bible Correspondence Course students were enrolled by "The Lutheran Hour" in Japan. The history in Korea was similar. In 1971, the sermonic format was added in Japan, Hoffmann says, because of "the intellectual bent of the Orient."

Financially "The Lutheran Hour" is on a sound footing. It has never solicited funds on the air. Thousands of sponsors in the Lutheran churches and the denominations of the wider Christian community underwrite the broadcast. Since there is no need to depend on listener support or denominational budgets, the broadcast can continue its $3,000,000 annual operation without fear.

The Back to God Hour

"The Lutheran Hour" had already established an extensive worldwide broadcasting system by the early 1940s when "The Back to God Hour," the radio voice of the Christian Reformed Church, was conceived. Modeling their operation in detail after "The Lutheran Hour," the creators of

"The Back to God Hour" even selected a radio preacher who looked, sounded, and thought much like Walter A. Maier—Peter Eldersveld, who developed the radio ministry of his denomination from its infancy on a local Chicago station to network distribution with Mutual and NBC. By his death in 1965 he had built a preaching staff of four, a foreign broadcast in three languages, and had moved beyond network distribution to a vigorous station-by-station syndication across the nation. Three hundred stations carried the program weekly to three million listeners. Two million copies of his sermon booklets were distributed each year. One hundred seventy thousand received his daily devotional booklet *The Family Altar*.

"The Back to God Hour" is noteworthy because of the breadth of its outreach by comparison with the size of the denomination that supports it, and because of the elaborate theological justification made for its preaching format. The Christian Reformed Church began in the United States in 1857 as the result of an immigration of a small number of Calvinists from the Netherlands into the Reformed Church in America, followed by the withdrawal of a few of these immigrants from the Reformed Church and affiliation on the part of two separatist pastors and a few small congregations. The denomination maintains direct ties with the Reformed churches of continental Europe. After a little over a century of existence, the Christian Reformed Church numbers 62,000 families or 300,000 total members. It invests about five million dollars annually in missions, besides a one and a half million dollar investment in "The Back to God Hour." Few denominations equal the per capita financial contributions of the Christian Reformed Church. In 1974 every family in the denomination was assessed $16.00 for support of the radio ministry.

The genius of the broadcast ministry of Eldersveld lay in his personal conviction about what he preached and his carefully honed skill in preaching it. He felt divinely called and providentially assigned to his task. His remarks on undertaking it are revealing:

> I am going to follow Paul's example as I take up this radio work. I cannot follow the customary radio technique. I have nothing to sell but I have something to tell. What is it? Nothing but the

> Gospel. I cannot agree with the writer of a certain book on Gospel broadcasting, whose underlying thought seems to be that we must adjust, mollify, and adapt the Gospel to our listeners, make it palatable enough to suit all of them, and avoid all controversial questions which might antagonize some of them. It strikes me that even in commercial radio it is hardly ethical for the advertiser to tell us anything but the truth about his product. But surely in religious radio work we must bear in mind that when we preach anything but the whole Gospel, or tone it down in deference to the listener, we are first of all making a liar of the God who sends us to speak for Him to the world, and secondly, we are doing a great injustice to the listener who needs the Gospel, whether he likes it or not.[14]

There can be no question that Eldersveld was a master of pulpit rhetoric. He was simply unacquainted with and thus suspicious of alternate religious program formats; indeed, the remarks above would suggest that he did not distinguish well between content and format.

It is one thing to maintain that the best mode of religious broadcasting is preaching. It is quite another thing to argue that any other format "tones down" the gospel and "makes a liar of God." Legitimate disgust for the commercial, profit-motivated deception of much contemporary spot advertising does not mean that it is impossible to broadcast honest, direct, clear, and scriptural radio and television spots.

Eldersveld urged that adapting the gospel broadcast to forms, techniques, and emphases with which the listeners are accustomed and to which they are attuned, mollifies them and compromises the message. At the same time, there have been few speakers who understood better than Eldersveld that cornerstone teaching of classical rhetoric: the need to know one's audience and frame one's words in terms that fit its circumstances. Within the confines of that rhetoric of which he was a master, he adapted to his audience with sensitivity and precision. Yet when it came to adapting to the framework of a wider audience through innovative broadcasting formats, Eldersveld argued that adaptation would be a compromise of the gospel.

The facts of the matter are these. Eldersveld was an

---

[14]Peter H. Eldersveld, *Nothing but the Gospel*, p. xix.

excellent preacher but he knew nothing about how to do other kinds of broadcasting. Preaching was cheap in production cost, while other formats tend to be costly. Preaching was easy to promote in his own denomination and in the "churched world" in general, and that is where the money and acclaim came from. Eldersveld's argument is thus completely understandable, if somewhat less than frank. His ministry depended financially on the popular and official support of the Christian Reformed Church. In that denomination the preaching of dogma has always had a central role. Eldersveld had to preserve credibility with his denominational supporters above all, and credibility for many of them meant a clear indication that the fixed doctrines of the Reformed theological tradition were being preached convincingly.

Already in 1928 the Christian Reformed Church had shown earnest interest in "preaching the Word" electronically. At the general synod meeting that year a concerted discussion of a radio ministry had included the following theological statement:

> The Church has been and should always be searching for ways and means whereby the great commission of Christ to preach the Gospel can be more effectively carried out; she should, therefore, welcome the means that promise to achieve this result more expeditiously. Now we have received the radio as a gift of God for that purpose. . . . Whereas there are millions to be reached, this work ought to be carried on in such a measure that the whole country is benefited thereby.[15]

Synod, however, did not decide to begin broadcasting a denominational program that year because of the size of the financial responsibility implied. The matter was not reconsidered in earnest until 1938. In 1939 "The Back to God Hour" was organized, but for the first half-dozen years, the program played intermittently throughout the year. No real radio audience was established since there was no continuity of the type that can be built on a regular broadcast with a single radio minister. Not until Eldersveld came into "The Back to God Hour" did the program become established as a regularly weekly pro-

---

[15]*Acts of Synod, Christian Reformed Church*, 1928, pp. 15f.

gram. Contracts with the Mutual and NBC networks were secured and the number of participating stations increased.

Eldersveld succeeded in giving permanence to the CRC radio ministry because he solved the problem of funding. Denominational assessments on each member family, freewill offering support, and occasional time concessions by networks and stations made the solution possible; Eldersveld's charisma made this support a reality.

In 1951 attempts were made to initiate television broadcasting. Between 1954 and 1956 three thirteen-week television series were authorized and funded, and two were filmed and aired. The first received excellent response. Though the second was substantially more sophisticated in broadcasting technique, it did not compete with the rapid advance in television broadcasting style and received only moderate station and audience appreciation. The effort was dropped.

Dr. Joel Nederhood, the present radio minister, joined "The Back to God Hour" staff in 1960 as a protégé of Eldersveld. He was joined by Spanish and Arabic broadcasting ministers in the early sixties, and by French and Chinese ministers in the seventies. During his early years with the radio ministry Nederhood spent considerable energy in follow-up work, cultivating the formation of groups of listeners in various areas, and attempting to encourage the development of new Christian Reformed congregations in areas of concentrated listener response. After the death of Eldersveld in 1965 Nederhood took the helm. His philosophy of Christian broadcasting corresponds to Eldersveld's and has continued to shape the radio ministry along those lines. Nederhood contends solidly for the preaching format, half-hour programs, and no television broadcasting.

Nederhood's beliefs about broadcast ministry are rooted in specific theological concepts of the church, mission, gospel, and proclamation. He defines the church in what he calls the "classic Reformed" sense. The church is the authoritative institution established by Christ and the apostles. It exists to speak for God to mankind in an authoritative proclamation of the truth about man's nature, need, duty, and destiny.[16] That proclamation demands obedience.

Such a definition of the church, Nederhood acknowledges, contrasts with the more prevalent notion of it as a volunteer fellowship, a human organization unified by a Christian spirit which exists to perform specific healing tasks and to improve the quality of human life by teaching and social reforms. Nederhood sees the church's authority as derived from its faithfulness to the apostolic witness. The Christian Reformed Church, he feels, has more profound authority than other churches because it is theologically more faithful to the apostolic witness. Its theological authenticity is a matter of its faithfulness to what the Bible says about God, man, and their relations. The church's authority depends, therefore, on the authority of Scripture, the truth from God. Because Scripture has absolute authority as divinely given and objective truth, the authority of a truly faithful church is absolute authority in teaching the truth.

The mission of a faithful church is to announce the truth and compel man to obedience to that truth. The church must make this announcement as an unqualified communication of "the truth," and it must do so by the most extensive and efficient means possible. The requisite proclamation and authority requires preaching, and broadcasting is an ideal tool for the authoritative announcement of the truth to mankind that preaching is.

Nederhood's concept of church and mission accurately represents the theological tradition of his denomination. It is a concept which implies that the church, as vicar of Christ, speaks with unqualified authority, asserting how men ought to answer large questions about the nature of life, self, morality, and meaning. This still leaves room for a view of the church as serving the real needs of humans, as defined by the church, but it lends that endeavor so authoritarian a cast as to obscure if not virtually eliminate the idea of church as a servant to the world, adapting itself to the actual needs that humans feel. It implies that the

---

[16]Personal interview with the author.

church begins with a theological prejudgment about where, morally and spiritually, humans are; where they must go; and precisely how all must achieve spiritual and moral maturity. Achieving the truth and insight is not a quest for mankind but a matter of adhering to established certainties. The church is "the pillar and ground of the truth" and preserves the "mysteries of God." Man's duty is to hear and adhere.

The definition of "truth" implied by the concept of church and mission that holds Nederhood to the preaching format is a broad one. It means the facts of the gospel applied to all aspects of human life. Mission is a declaration of how the claim of Christ on man relates to and shapes every facet of his life and culture. The "Christ claim," however, is a claim on the spiritual attitudes and experiences of people. These in turn presumably shape man's conduct and culture. Mission, therefore, is not the church's adaptation of its ministry to those social, economic, moral, and political needs that shape the quality of human life. The definition of mission "must be controlled by one's concept of the church, rather than by one's concept or view of the world," according to Nederhood.

So to define church and mission shapes one's concept of proclamation. The good news of the gospel is the truth about substitutionary atonement and the mystical presence of God's Holy Spirit in humans. Proclamation is conceived as the communication of that truth through authoritative preaching. Since the church has the truth, since it knows the answers to man's problem, its mission is to announce authoritatively that true answer, and thus compel man to conform to the truth; and that announcement is proclamation.

The proclamation, on Nederhood's view, must be verbal, because that is the form of communication he believes God used. It must be a declaration. It is never a quest, inquiry, or suggestion. It is not open-ended in character. Other methods than the spoken word might possibly be proclamatory in a secondary sense, but they lack the authority and precision of the spoken word. Perhaps, he concedes, proclamation could be defined in degrees of authenticity. Preaching would be the first degree. A written message would be the second degree. Religious drama might be the third degree.

What Nederhood says about church, mission, gospel, and proclamation has significant consequences for broadcasting media. Radio and television function with varied effectiveness in that task. There is little regard on this view for Marshall McLuhan's notions about the "media as message" or the "media as massage." Nederhood does not pay a great deal of attention to how the medium conditions the message impact people get. The medium is merely the tool for pictures or words, a tool that can be employed—more or less effectively—for preaching. Obviously, Nederhood's position is a more sophisticated theological statement of Eldersveld's objections to adapting the format of a religious broadcast to audience habits or preference.

In recent years Nederhood has allowed some variation in the amount and length of preaching; and programs of thirty, fifteen, five, and one minutes have been aired. There has also been some testing of interview programs and musical variety shows. These still constitute rare exceptions, not aired in areas where there is a concentration of "preaching-oriented" Christian Reformed supporters.

The cost of television broadcasting is formidable, probably beyond the means of the Christian Reformed Church. Even if the money were available, Nederhood would be likely to avoid television and use the money to purchase more air time on radio. He is unenthusiastic about the prospects of using television for religious broadcasting. The disadvantage, he feels, is the cultural role and character of television. As it has developed in the United States particularly, television is an entertainment medium, not a message medium. Proclamation, as defined by "The Back to God Hour," can never afford to be confused with entertainment because the former is essentially demanding and instructional:

> Even after you have produced a successful show, in terms of the ministry of the church, you still have to ask the question, "What have we done?" Even though you may have come across with certain biblical information, certain moral material and that type of thing, you've still used an entertainment medium to project this information. So the question in my mind is always, "What

has the ultimate effect been?" Has it been simply that a man has relaxed in front of the TV screen for ten or fifteen minutes?

There are a number of problems in such a view of the television medium. One might argue that there is no *better* context in which to inform humans than that of relaxed entertainment. Paul Stevens' documentary on the archaeology of Palestine and its relevance to the Christian message was aired on network prime time with great effect, suggesting that television can allow for good proclamation. And even if proclamation is limited—on Nederhood's own terms—to authoritatively verbalizing information, is there a better matrix for it than the relaxing, audio-visual presentation of information couched in a striking dramatic technique like that of the Lutheran "This Is the Life?"

At another level, one could make a strong case for a theology of the church radically different from that of Eldersveld and Nederhood. One could argue that the Bible defines the church as servant, with the mandate of adapting to any human situation so as to improve the quality of total human existence. On such an understanding, flexibility would be the hallmark of the church, rather than authority. Truth would be seen as a matter of a continuing, active quest, rather than mere appropriation of established answers. Mission would be viewed as the incitement in persons and society of growth toward love and graciousness, by whatever means it works. Christianity would be a matter of behavioral function rather than mystical or intellectual posture.

If such a theology of the church were adopted, any form of effective communication would be proclamation if it succeeded in getting across to someone the insight that incites him to spiritual relief and personal freedom; that induces behavior that is forgiveness incarnated; that renews and reshapes him in the image of Christ. Perhaps that kind of proclamation would be in the form of a sensation, or an impression, or an emotion, or a concrete concept. It might be communicated by word, picture, or sound. Certainly it is not restricted to verbally incited intellectual process.

Human orientations, needs, problems, and predilections, it might be argued, should shape the format of broadcasting and determine what is communicated. The message and method of the church's mission must start in the world, not in the Word; must start with man's predicament, not with a predestined divine construction of "truth." In the New Testament, God's truth is the announcement of grace, shaped and tailored in terms of the character and location of the human situation. It is not a deposit of truth. It is the dynamic of a true life. It is not God-centered but man-centered.

Such a model of proclamation is considerably broader than that which, while reflecting its tradition accurately, has shaped the successes of "The Back to God Hour."

Charles E. Coughlin

A new prosperity grew up in America in the half-dozen years following the First World War. In those "roaring twenties," economics, freedom, social awareness, and international interest were in the minds of Americans. In Detroit the Ford Motor Company had expanded, its industrial development creating a social phenomenon that has since become commonplace—the suburb. Once-distant small towns were progressively absorbed into expanding metropolitan areas. Urbanization and suburban development brought the Canadian-born priest Father Charles E. Coughlin to Royal Oak, Michigan, in 1926.

Royal Oak was becoming aware of its role as an upper middle class residential element of the Detroit metropolis, and the Roman Catholic diocese of Detroit sensed the potential for church expansion. When the thirty-five-year-old priest arrived in Royal Oak, his parish numbered twenty-five families, and he was unknown. Seven years later he had an American audience of 45,000,000. He was to be credited as the "one man most responsible for the election of Franklin D. Roosevelt to the presidency." He had his own political lobby of five million members, and succeeded in flooding Congress with 200,000 telegrams as a result of one speech. One of his sermons netted him 1,200,000 letters.[17] Relying solely on the spoken word

---

[17] D. T. Coe, "A Rhetorical Study of Selected Radio Speeches of Reverend Charles E. Coughlin," pp. vii, 22, 33; see also Erik Barnouw, *The Golden Web*, p. 44.

MODELS OF RELIGIOUS BROADCASTING

and the power of broadcasting, he became a major political force in the United States.

Coughlin was born of Irish descent on October 25, 1891, in Hamilton, Ontario. He came from a considerable line of devout Catholic laboring people. His father became sexton of the Hamilton Cathedral. He was educated in Toronto at St. Michael's College and University College, and graduated with honors in philosophy. Ordained in 1916, he went on to teach at Assumption College in Ontario. In February 1923 he was received into the Detroit diocese.

Within a few days of his arrival at his new parish in May 1926, Coughlin had apparently conceived the idea of expanding his impact beyond those few families by means of radio. He visited WJR to discuss the children's religious instruction programs he proposed to broadcast to Royal Oak. By August 15 Coughlin announced to his constituency that the parish of the "Little Flower," Saint Theresa, would have a radio ministry.

> It was a thunderbolt to these staid parishioners. They were conservative men.... Broadcasting was expensive. Broadcasting was treacherous. Broadcasting was a novelty. Broadcasting was irreligious. More than all, these gentlemen did not feel capable of supporting even the ordinary burdens of a parish, let alone this extraordinary and unprofitable expenditure which would be more appropriately undertaken to advertise cigarettes and soap and motor cars than to disseminate the principles of Christianity.[18]

Nonetheless, the broadcast started in October 1926 on air time given free by WJR. Line hookup cost $58.00 per program. Coughlin preached from the shrine at 3:00 p.m. on October 17. His audience had grown from twenty-five families to the population of southeast Michigan. The broadcast continued weekly for exactly three years, expanding in 1929 with the addition of stations WMAQ and WLW of Chicago and Cincinnati. In 1930 CBS signed a contract to carry his radio message. The following year an independent chain of stations was developed to carry Coughlin from the Mississippi to the Atlantic.

The broadcast was costing Coughlin $14,000 a week in

---

[18] Louis B. Ward, *Father Charles E. Coughlin*, p. 16.

PULPITS AND PROPHETS

1931; but within a year he had achieved the audience of forty-five million. By 1934 his mail exceeded that of every other human being. *Fortune* magazine called him "the biggest thing that ever happened to radio." In the succeeding years his fame and impact peaked. Then a negative remark he broadcast about Roosevelt—calling him stupid for appointing to the Supreme Court Hugo Black, a former member of the Ku Klux Klan—sent reverberations through the higher echelons of church and government across the nation. The Bishop of Detroit reprimanded Coughlin. Coughlin cancelled his broadcasts. A year later, in November 1938, he returned to the air. Things went badly this time around. He gained an anti-semitic reputation for a pro-Nazi speech broadcast November 20, 1938. He continued to attack the President as he proposed his simple, socialist solutions to the pain of the depression.

The Social Justice Publishing Company, which he had established, turned out voluminous "follow-up" literature, but Coughlin's reputation had been tarnished badly across the nation. The Roman Catholic hierarchy offered decreasing support. The forces were marshaled to shut him down. The National Association of Broadcasters drafted a strict new code, which

> prohibited all "controversial speakers" from buying air time on the radio unless they appeared on a panel and other views were also presented. One official of the National Association of Broadcasters sent a letter to all radio stations asking them to advise the National headquarters if they were carrying Coughlin's broadcasts. Stations were to respond with dates of contracts' expiration, what provisions were provided for cancellations, and whether renewal broadcast contracts had been offered or accepted. The code, which did not refer to Coughlin by name, was obviously directed at him.[19]

Coughlin's finances reflected his declining influence: $574,416 in 1938, $102,254 in 1939, $82,263 in 1940. But Coughlin was not yet ready to throw in the towel. His newspaper, *Social Justice*, called for the impeachment of President Roosevelt; he blew hot and cold for Willkie; and he continued to blame the Jews for the economic problems of the United States and European war.

[19] Coe, *op. cit.*, p. 145.

MODELS OF RELIGIOUS BROADCASTING

By the end of 1941 Coughlin found it nearly impossible to renew his broadcasting contracts. In the late spring of 1942 the government invoked the Espionage Act of 1917 against him. Coughlin was called before the archbishop and offered the choice of terminating his paper *Social Justice* or leaving the office of priesthood. He chose to remain a priest. On May 4 the Postmaster General revoked his license for *Social Justice*.

Coughlin was bitter over the loss of his enormous listening audience and extensive press coverage, but he stayed with his parish, which had grown considerably and continued to do so. But though he remained in good standing in the church, he disappeared from public view. By the time of his retirement in 1968 Father Coughlin was not a political force even in Royal Oak. He looked back on the early 1940s with humility. He admitted that it had been difficult for him to go from a national orator to a parish preacher and priest, but said of those earlier days:

> I committed an egregious error, which I am the first to admit, when I permitted myself to attack persons. I could never bring myself to philosophize the morality of that now. It was a young man's mistake.[20]

Coughlin was primarily an orator. Broadcasting for him meant preaching, and to many people he seemed relevant to the end as he addressed himself to the hopes and fears gripping the nation.[21] Coughlin thought that religion was supposed to improve the quality of the life of people, so he grappled with the forces that seemed to him to be despoiling that life.

> His subject matter involved a diversity of political strands, stemming from varied sources. Sometimes he spoke of the perils of communism, the "red serpent." Sometimes he pleaded for the remonetization of silver, and sounded like a Populist leader of the turn of the century. More often he castigated those of wealth and power, "dulled by the opiate of their own contentedness." As the Depression began this became the dominant theme.[22]

[20]Bernard Eesinoun, "Reflections of a Radio Priest," *Focus Mid-West*, Feb. 1963, pp. 8-10.
[21]Barnouw, *The Golden Web*, p. 45.
[22]*Ibid.*

PULPITS AND PROPHETS

Regardless of his judgment, style, or timing, he was undeniably a man of conviction in his endeavor to change the conditions of human pain. Coughlin favored controlled capitalism, and insisted that human rights took priority over commercial and property rights. Those suffering from the Depression liked what they heard.

Coughlin was credible to the common man, mainly because of his appeal to simple logic. He started with the facts that bit into people's daily lives, not with abstract theological ideas. Like Bishop Sheen later, he focused on the pain and passion of real people. In the midst of political confusion, economic deprivation, social anxiety, and spiritual dissatisfaction, he argued simply and logically, always ending with a specific course of action that the individual could undertake. He persuaded his audience to vote, send mail, wire Congress, protest, boycott, or support. His listeners understood what they could do and they did it.

Perhaps the most significant single force in shaping Coughlin's ministry was Pope Leo XIII's encyclical *Rerum Novarum*. This famous papal document, issued in the year of Coughlin's birth, painted Christianity as a force demanding humane social reformation. It was when Coughlin discovered that encyclical that he was motivated to become a priest. Though he often seemed radical in his persuasion, what he championed can readily be seen as a reflection of *Rerum Novarum*.

In pursuit of the ideals of *Rerum Novarum* Coughlin followed a style as old as Greece and Rome. What made Cicero a great orator two millennia ago was the stuff that made Coughlin's oratory convincing and attractive.

> Coughlin ... successfully employed motivational appeals to gain the attention of his audience, suggest courses of action, and motivate his listeners toward predetermined objectives. His use of motivational appeals is further evidence of the classical rhetorical position that the effective speaker must have a knowledge of his audience's emotional behavior.... He spoke to the needs of his day: and his words were attended to, appreciated and—above all—*acted upon*.[23]

He prepared his radio discourses meticulously, often work-

---

[23] Coe, *op. cit.*, abstract.

MODELS OF RELIGIOUS BROADCASTING

ing throughout the night before broadcast. He had a natural fluency, a rolling Irish "r", and brilliance in English speech and literature. As one biographer wrote, "He had a rare command of the language. He chose his words with infinite discretion—hand-picked plums of wisdom. His diction presupposed practiced elocution."[24]

Coughlin wrote out his discourses in detail in advance and read them from the prepared text. When he read, his whole personality seemed to overflow.

> His distinction: a voice of such mellow richness, such manly, heartwarming, confidential intimacy, such emotional and ingratiating charm, that anyone tuning past it almost automatically returned to hear it again. It was without doubt one of the great speaking voices of the twentieth century. Warmed by the touch of Irish brogue it lingered over words and enriched their emotional content. It was a voice made for promises.[25]

While he spoke, Coughlin would often summarize what he had already said, and outline what he was going to conclude. His talks were full of illustrations and appeals to Americanism, love, self-preservation, nostalgia, and honor. He quoted extensively from Scripture, described what evils would ensue if his counsel were neglected, and called his hearers to act. He used fear and anxiety, excited by the pictures he painted of life, to persuade people to do something. There was sufficient reason for the American people to be afraid of the evil that social neglect, political irresponsibility, and public immorality can bring upon a society and its culture. While Roosevelt was poetically romanticizing that there was nothing to fear but fear itself, Coughlin knew that there were plenty of homely things that the people did fear—starving children, ruined industry, deadly war, killing crime, spiritual waste, and personal loss of meaning. Coughlin was their priest and he tried to find a way for them.

Unfortunately he was only a man—and he was still young—and he made serious errors of judgment. But he was *for* the people and *for* Christ; and he probably under-

---

[24] Ruth Mugglebee, *Father Coughlin of the Shrine of the Little Flower*, p. 29.

[25] Isabel Leighton (ed.), *The Aspirin Age, 1919-41*, p. 234.

stood that to risk action, even when the way is unclear, is faith, while refusing to act, for safety's sake, is unbelief.

Bob Shuler

Sheen's reputation was built from an East Coast base. Maier and Hoffmann, Eldersveld and Nederhood, and Coughlin represent the Midwest and Middle America. The West Coast has also produced a spate of religious broadcasters. California turned out such well-known stars in the religious radio firmament as Charles E. Fuller, Herbert W. Armstrong, Aimee Semple McPherson, and Bob Shuler.

The friends of the Reverend Robert Pierce Shuler called him "Savanarola in Los Angeles." His foes said he was the "Holy Terror." He was born in Virginia in 1880. The setting was rural and, by today's standards, deprived.

> He was eight years old when he saw his first town, his first railroad train, his first Negro, and his first daily newspaper. He graduated from Emory & Henry College, a remote Blue Ridge intellectual smelter whose authorities characteristically ordained him to preach the mysteries of Southern Methodism three years before he received his AB, and the same year he received his varsity letter in football.[26]

After a series of minor Texas pastorates, he was appointed university pastor at the University of Texas in Austin. He waded into local politics and corruption with righteous fury and the governor and a senator resigned their offices in consequence.

By his own account, Shuler was banished from Austin on September 27, 1920. He headed for Los Angeles, where he wasted no time in getting the press firmly focused on his ministry and person. He never lost its attention until his departure from religious broadcasting in late 1933. According to Martin Neeb, there were more than 475 articles about Shuler in the *Los Angeles Times* between 1927 and 1933. The burden of Shuler's preaching remained essentially the same throughout his popular days in the church and on radio: the pulpit was the place for

---

[26]Ray Duncan, "Fighting Bob Shuler—the Holy Terror," *Los Angeles Magazine*, VIII, No. 3, p. 38.

MODELS OF RELIGIOUS BROADCASTING

exposés of sin and corruption. But words are cheap, and a person must act out his commitment in "picturesque conduct rather than language."[27]

Shuler's pulpit style increased his congregation to six thousand, and *Bob Shuler's Magazine* began monthly publication in 1926. On October 5, 1926, Shuler accepted Lizzie Glide's gift of radio station KGEF, which was installed in the tower of his church. By the end of the year he was reaching millions.

Shuler's programs were heard three days a week. Sunday included an hour of Bible instruction, two hours of preaching services, and a half-hour of music. Wednesday featured an hour of children's instruction, forty-five minutes of adult instruction, an hour of music, and an hour of discussion with Shuler conducted through written questions that had been submitted. On Friday a half-hour of Bible instruction led to a half-hour of music and an address by Shuler on the life of the community.

The programs that drew the phenomenal attention Shuler enjoyed were the sermons and the Friday civic messages. Both tended to be racy and invited the audience to identify with Bob Shuler, the invader of dens of iniquity. Typical was his exposé of a party, apparently held by a thousand "Christians," who were "celebrating the coming of our Lord engaged in a drunken carousal, with hugging, kissing, in drunken fashion, women displaying their nakedness, brazenly, openly, flagrantly, and viciously, with booze sold openly contrary to law, and the most suggestive dancing engaged in."[28] The *American Mercury* declared that Shuler was "hotter news than murder."[29]

Shuler used his power to force a police chief out of office, elect a reform mayor, imprison a district attorney, and so affect the metropolis that he was accused of being a dictator, not only of the morals and manners but also the politics of Los Angeles. It was said that "no politician dares oppose Bob Shuler, and no politician even dares run

---

[27] Martin J. Neeb, "An Historical Study of American Non-Commercial AM Broadcast Stations Owned and Operated by Religious Groups, 1920-1966," p. 30.
[28] *Ibid.*
[29] Duncan Aikman, "Savanarola in Los Angeles," *American Mercury*, Vol. XI, No. 84, p. 424.

for office if he has ever lunched publicly with a woman not his wife."[30]

Shuler operated on intuition. He did not need the facts if he knew he was right. His methodology for acquiring information, executing his attack, and generally using people ran roughshod over the standards of Christian ethics—and occasionally over the laws of the land. He was fined or jailed several times for contempt of court. Although his radio coverage had expanded throughout the Southwest by 1930, opposition to his arbitrary and superficial moralism had also begun to rise. In 1930 the Federal Radio Commission took action against his dissemination of "private gossip" on public airways, and in November 1931 terminated his license to broadcast (a Court of Appeals confirmed the decision in 1933). In 1932 he lost a bid for the United States Senate. Thereafter, his power faded. Neeb writes:

> Although he remained a prominent figure in Los Angeles until 1953 when he stepped down from his pulpit to retire, his influence was limited. In his final sermon before his people he said, "I have been a scrapper for God."[31]

The "Scrapper for God" had acquired the twentieth-century tools with which to carry out what he saw as his "divine task." The common folk were attracted by his cheap and sensationalist moralizing. But the institutions of American justice balanced the accounts, and the preacher finally had to bow to responsible propriety.

Bits and Pieces

Other religious broadcasters too numerous to mention have received national attention, sometimes engaging huge audiences, since 1925. Those who have employed the electronic media as a pulpit have tended consistently to follow the model and format of the broadcasters discussed in this chapter. Some mild forms of innovation have been employed within the pulpit model, in an effort to overcome the consistent problem of reaching the unchurched.

---

[30] Quoted by Duncan, *op. cit.*, p. 66.
[31] Neeb, *op. cit.*, p. 75.

MODELS OF RELIGIOUS BROADCASTING

The late Bob Meyers employed a variety of poetry, romantically evangelical music, and a nautical flavor for his "Good Ship Grace" broadcast. But his "eight bells and all is well" suggested a world scene that makes sense only to a certain mildly mystical brand of Christian. His essentially "fundamentalist" constituency apparently liked the flavor and feeling, but it did not reach the unchurched. Charles E. Fuller's "Old Fashioned Revival Hour" was popular with traditionally churched Presbyterians of an unusually conservative bent. He appealed to evangelicals who especially enjoyed a supernaturalist picture of life and destiny. Though he reached a large number of American homes from Long Beach, the "Old Fashioned Revival Hour" remained old-fashioned, and was never clearly related to the twentieth century in the mind of the unchurched and pragmatic American.

M. R. De Haan's "Radio Bible Class," from Grand Rapids, tended to a "pseudo-pedagogical" format. It made an attempt to engage the audience in the interchange of "discussion," but the format wavered between preaching and teaching—with the latter oriented to the committed religious American accustomed to the sermonic communication. Herbert W. Armstrong and son Garner Ted present a unique preaching form on "The World Tomorrow." At first hearing, it is difficult to discern exactly what sort of program one is tuned to. The Armstrongs (their voices are difficult to distinguish) make an overt attempt to employ a vocal style like Paul Harvey. The organization of material content, paragraph and sentence style, illustration, and figures of speech are virtually indistinguishable from that of the news comentator.

The standard of excellence for broadcast preaching is comparison with the "National Radio Pulpit." In the consistent quality of its programming and in sheer durability, it far exceeds all other similar programs. Begun in 1923, it is still aired weekly with popular acclaim. From its advent as a national broadcast in 1926, it has featured outstanding American pulpiteers. S. Parkes Cadman set the precedent for color and clarity in content and delivery. The precedent became a tradition as he was followed by Harry Emerson Fosdick, Ralph Sockman, and David H. C. Read.

PULPITS AND PROPHETS

All these worthies of major American pulpits are among the supremely effective preachers of the twentieth century, and they made the electronic media serve impressively as pulpit.

Three elements have consistently been present in preaching broadcasts and three elements in the follow-up ministries. The broadcasts regularly include music, an announcer, and the preacher with his sermon. The function of the music is, with rare exceptions, to set the stage, to move the audience into the broadcast. Music is strictly a mood-setting device in the "preaching model" religious broadcast. The announcer functions similarly, but he focuses specifically on setting up the audience for the preacher. Generally, his task is to establish the preacher's authority and credibility quickly and efficiently in the listener's subconscious.

As we have suggested, in the pulpit model of religious broadcasting the preacher *is* the program. For the most part, the history of broadcast preaching is an account of religious partisanship. The task of organizing and funding an enormous enterprise like a national preaching broadcast is apparently so formidable that only those who are driven by overwhelming private and personal ambition can achieve success at it. That ambition may be wholesome—as in Sheen's case—or pathological—as with Shuler—but in either case it tends to be associated with and draw its vigor from partisanship.

The more adamantly partisan and sensational the preacher, the larger his audience has tended to be. His sensationalism may have lain in scandal, as with Shuler and Bob Harrington (the "chaplain of Bourbon Street"); or in complicated doctrine, as with Fuller and Nederhood; or in fear-mongering, as with Coughlin and the Armstrongs.

Maier, Hoffmann, Eldersveld, and the preachers of the "National Radio Pulpit" are exceptions to this. Their strength has been in their sensitive assessment of human suffering and their carefully reasoned theistic prescription for it. While these latter preachers have had stable and sizable audiences, their command of national attention has seldom approached that of the sensationalists.

The three forms of follow-up in broadcast preaching

have been instructional literature, local rallies, and a regularly published "magazine." Response to the follow-up materials has generally been one basis for evaluating the effectiveness of the broadcast, though the most commonly cited criterion is the number of letters received. These letters tend to be from committed Christians, committed churchmen, or committed religionists. If the objective of the broadcast is to reinforce the commitment of the committed, then "letters-per-broadcast" is a valid standard of evaluation of the program's success—though it does not, of course, answer the question of whether the money used to produce it might have been spent more wisely. If, however, the purpose of the broadcast is to make the gospel an authentic option to the unchurched, un-Christian, unreligious people in the listening audience, then the "letters-per-broadcast" judgment is of little value as a method of evaluation.

No matter how skillful or popular broadcasting preachers have been, the use of electronic mass media for preaching remains problematic. The Sheens, the Maiers, the Fosdicks have sometimes overcome the media problem by their sheer heroic quality as people. But when broadcast religion has followed the pulpit model, it has modeled the prophets of the Old Testament. Preaching as a communications technique stands in contrast to communication by incarnation. The opening verses of the Letter to the Hebrews indicate the contrast between the method of revelation and communication in the Old Testament prophets, and that in the New Testament with the coming of the Messiah: "God, who in bits and pieces at sporadic intervals spoke to the fathers by the prophets, has in these last days spoken unto us in His Son."

The difference between the techniques used at the two different historical periods is the difference between the act of a transcendent, absent God and of an immanent, present God. Preaching models the prophet who speaks *for* and thus *about* God, rather than enacting God's character and presence. Preaching subconsciously implies an inaccurate image of God's character. It implies that emphasis is to be placed on God's transcendence rather than his incarnation; that he stands outside of man's life and authoritatively imposes on it; that he announces his wisdom and will to a subservient race. This contrasts radically with the good news of the New Testament, which would insist that God is of such a character that he has visited and is visiting men as a friend. It is uniquely Christ's relationship with people which expresses and reveals divine grace. In that enacted sense he *is* the Word. The contrasting idea of revelation *primarily* by words is a confluence of the Old Testament prophetic tradition of announcement in the name of the feudal king or overlord on the one hand, and the Greek idea that salvation is by wisdom on the other.

The difficulties of that concept of communicating the Christian gospel have become abundantly evident in the last two thousand years in the congregational setting. The relatively small proportion of what the preacher had in mind that is really communicated to the congregation is appalling. How much more is efficient communication normally jeopardized when the added distance of the broadcast medium is introduced! In the congregational setting, at least, the preacher can, to some degree, become actor. At the least, he is there as a presence with his people. But the broadcast preacher is personally removed from his audience and—with the possible rare exception of the genuine personality cult figure—cannot be "incarnate" communication for them.

Moreover, preaching can imply an extremely ungenerous view of man and God. It suggests by its very style that man is intellect, who needs *announcement* of a kind of "Greek" wisdom or Old Testament "ecstasy," by which he may be convicted, convinced, and changed. The process is more suggestive of manipulation than growth. God is supernaturalized into a position from which at best he "shepherds" man imperiously and at worst commands him. Such a model poorly reflects Christ's incarnate visitation of his "brothers and sisters and mother" (Matt. 12:46-50).

Christ's intent was clearly that the church's communication techniques conform to his. The church was commissioned by the New Testament to "proclaim," not necessarily to "preach," and above all to be the continuing incarnation in each generation. The pulpit model of proclaiming is the Old Testament model of the prophet. Is there perhaps a better, New Testament, model for communication as incarnation today?[32]

---

[32]See J. Harold Ellens, "Creative Worship," *CAPS Proceedings* 1970 for a further discussion of preaching, proclamation, incarnation and communication of the gospel.

four
Sinai and the Spectacular

If broadcast preaching models the prophets, as we suggested in the preceding chapter, Billy Graham models Mount Sinai. Preaching is not the primary part of the program for Graham. His impact is in the crusade spectacular he creates. The same is true for such figures as Rex Humbard and Oral Roberts. Preaching is important for all of them, but its significance in their broadcasts is in the role it plays in the total spectacle. The desired audience effect hangs not on the preaching, but on the total package.

The staging for these spectacles is costly and magnificent, including dramatic music, awesome settings, careful psychological timing, suave leading to the sermon, vigorous rhetoric, and altar calls with the ensuing procession of penitents coming forward. The television set becomes a window on this "mighty act of God."

MODELS OF RELIGIOUS BROADCASTING

Preaching has a part in such a "mighty act" comparable to the role Moses played in the Sinai spectacular three thousand years ago. The spectacle is not so much using camera and microphone to extend the pulpit as it is an electronic view of an Old Testament "invasion" of God into our lives and history. Graham, Roberts, and Humbard demonstrate in their technically brilliant *shows* that God acts in personal and public history today as at the creation, the Exodus, and Sinai. The suggestion is that God acts *through his prophets*, Humbard, Roberts, and Graham, who serve as catalysts to the contemporary "mighty acts of God" needed to redeem this wretched world.

The religious broadcast spectacle did not wait for the advent of television, however. An amazing woman attuned religious radio to the "mighty acts of God" model half a century ago. Aimee Semple McPherson, with "The Four Square Gospel" in Los Angeles, staged a new "Mt. Sinai" every week. She made the supernatural God seem a natural part of this world of time and space. For audiences across the nation, she made redemptive divine intervention in history and in the individual's life seem possible.

Aimee Semple McPherson

Aimee was born on a farm in Ingersoll, Ontario, in 1890. At the age of seventeen, she was converted and baptized by an evangelist who was to become her husband the next year. She and her husband began a ministry as traveling evangelists. Though she had no theological training, she was ordained at 18, and became a strong force in her husband's ministry in Canada, the United States, Ireland, Great Britain, and China.

When Robert Semple died of malaria in China in 1910, Aimee continued the work, achieving remarkably greater heights of "success" than before. "By 1918 she was drawing such crowds from Maine to Florida that tent-cities were being built to hold the followers and she was renting the largest halls in the city for her meetings."[1] She married

---

[1] Neeb, "An Historical Study of American Non-Commercial AM Broadcast Stations, 1920-1966," p. 114.

SINAI AND THE SPECTACULAR

Harold McPherson in 1913 and was divorced from him in 1921. Her final marriage was in 1931 to David Hutton, but it had little significance for her public life.

An evangelistic campaign in Denver packed the 12,000-seat auditorium there every night for three weeks, and Aimee's spectacular "invasion" of the West had begun. Ten thousand answered the altar calls. Hundreds were brought in for healing. The campaign was marked by "numerous miracles." Later she moved on to California, conducting campaigns in the San Francisco area and in Los Angeles. The name she gave her ministry struck her one night as she preached on "Christ's four-fold ministry as Savior, Baptizer, Healer, and Coming King"—the gospel, she suddenly exclaimed, is *foursquare*.[2]

As her fame increased, her wealth did as well. She built a cathedral in Los Angeles as the central temple for her broadly ranging ministry, financing it with offerings from her campaigns in the cities of America.[3] Built at a cost of $1.5 million, the Angelus Temple seated 5300. It was topped by the largest unsupported dome in the United States, and graced with stained glass competitive in quality to that in European cathedrals. It opened with the New Year in 1923. At first Aimee preached every night and three times on Sunday to capacity crowds. Attendance reached 50,000 per week and offerings were often $10,000 a service. Just over a year later she began a nationwide radio broadcast from the Temple.

Aimee had mastered theatrical techniques in her campaigns. She burned her mortgage standing atop her church while 15,000 people watched. Her proclamation consisted of "living sermons" with exquisite stage sets for each service. She recognized the value of constant press coverage. Given her flair for communicating, it is no surprise that she soon translated her success electronically. Aimee understood radio thoroughly and knew that she could make it work as a dramatic medium for her message and

---

[2] "The Church of the Foursquare Gospel," *Four Square*, May 1954, p. 15.
[3] Aimee Semple McPherson, "On My Fortieth Anniversary. A Brief History of the Foursquare Gospel."

MODELS OF RELIGIOUS BROADCASTING

her personality. She said at the outset of her broadcasting career:

> It has now become possible to stand in the pulpit, and speaking in a normal voice, reach hundreds of thousands of listeners.... We fully expect to reach with the preached word the prairie wife with her little family; the mountaineer amid the rugged crag and timbers of his alpine abode; the desert dweller amidst the sand dunes, cactus and sage brush; the Indian chief ... ; the blue jacket who sails in Uncle Sam's warships; the cripple in the wheelchair; the businessman as he sits at his luncheon.[4]

But she realized that she could not be effective without careful attention to what she was doing. Her station was always outfitted with the finest equipment. She designed her system to broadcast from the Temple auditorium or a parlor studio. Aimee saw the two antenna towers symbolically as the two arms of her sanctuary, eternally lifted 250 feet toward God, "alive, tingling, pulsing spires of steel, mute witnesses that at Angelus Temple every moment of the day and night, a silent and invisible messenger awaits the command to carry, on the winged feet of the winds, the story of hope, the words of joy, of comfort, of salvation."[5]

Aimee Semple McPherson's impact over the radio prevailed for twenty years, surviving her divorce and unproven rumors about her. As late as 1942 it was still so large that the *Los Angeles Times* could state, "A world war is the only thing that could have reduced Aimee Semple McPherson to an inside page position."[6]

A description of the imaginative drama she developed to communicate a baptismal service to her radio audience illustrates well the spectacle she created. A microphone was placed near the edge of the baptistery. The sounds of her voice, the splashing water, and the exhilaration of the newly baptized could be heard. As many as a hundred a week were baptized by Aimee. White-robed they went down into the water to become "dead to sin."

> "Oh, what a happy funeral!" cries the priestess. Curtains part upon an elaborate scene of palms, flowers and grassy banks,

---

[4]*Four Square*, Dec. 1923, p. 24.
[5]*Ibid.*, p. 18.
[6]*Los Angeles Times*, Oct. 9, 1942, p. 232.

SINAI AND THE SPECTACULAR

below which water ripples enticingly.... "This sister is seventy-seven years old, bless her!" The pinched little white face strains up to the surface again, white hair matted "Praise Him, hallelujah!"[7]

The spectacle was meticulously, mysteriously described for radio listeners, who were transfixed by the dramatic process.

Aimee encouraged her radio audience to kneel next to their radios for prayer with her. She invited them to place their hands on the radio receiver for a sense of contact and presence. She soothed and "tuned" them with gentle hymns and familiar religious phrases. Her people wept and prayed and supported her ministry richly and joyfully. Aimee emphasized that her broadcast was not meant to entertain or to "lull them to sleep with the sweet strains of the organ,"[8] but to save souls and to heal bodies through the medium of radio.[9] Her radio spectaculars were miraculous. Hundreds of thousands of people were electrified with the certainty that the broadcasts represented God's invasion into their personal lives. Thousands believed they were miraculously healed.

Aimee's imagination worked constantly. In 1925 Angelus Temple entered a great float into the Tournament of Roses Parade. Strategically located throughout it were radio receivers tuned to KFSG. As the float rolled through Pasadena it "flung the Gospel message upon the winds."[10] The crowds were thrilled. The Angelus Temple float took the Sweepstakes trophy.

That summer Aimee launched a great crusade. Evangelists were commissioned for an extensive tent ministry in a variety of places reached by Aimee's broadcast. A two-way radio hookup enabled all the congregations gathered in the far-flung tents to join in worship with the congregation at Angelus Temple.

> When a hymn number was given out in the Temple, the congregation in these various cities opened their hymnals to the same

---

[7] Sarah Comstock, "Aimee Semple McPherson—Prima Donna of Revivalism," *Harper's Magazine* (Dec. 1927), p. 14.
[8] Neeb, *op. cit.*, p. 141.
[9] *The Bridal Call Foursquare*, June 1926, p. 32.
[10] Neeb, *op. cit.*, p. 135.

number; ... When one was told to lift their hands, all lifted their hands; when one congregation was asked to wave their handkerchiefs, they all waved together; all listened to the same sermon, and the leaves of Bibles turned and rustled simultaneously in the various cities; ... when the aisles of the Temple were choked with men and women coming forward to kneel in penitence at the Savior's feet, the aisles of the tents saw similar lines coming forward to bow at the foot of the Cross.[11]

Aimee would receive the newly penitent into membership in Angelus Temple. Their confession came by radio. She addressed them invitingly with the words:

"Do you believe in the Inspiration of the Scripture? In the Virgin Birth? In the atonement?" The Temple audience gasped in amazement, then cheered loudly, when the answer came back, "I do!" from a chorus of voices. The response came from a telephone installed at her elbow, amplified at KFSG, and broadcast into the Temple auditorium and out over radio to be heard thousands of miles away. Thus were the first members received into a church by means of radio.[12]

Rex Humbard

The stage for Rex Humbard's international evangelism spectacular is the Cathedral of Tomorrow in Cuyahoga Falls, Ohio, but his arena is the whole world.

Though Humbard has never had any formal theological training, though his ordination was by his traveling evangelist father, though he belongs to no denomination, he has been preaching the gospel for forty years and is now pastor of the world's largest interdenominational church.

Rex Humbard, a native of Little Rock, Arkansas, is the son of A. E. Humbard, who was a vigorous evangelist for 53 years. The son, oldest of six children, began his life work as part of the Humbard Family Singers. As the group became well known, they began to appear on radio programs, gradually building a sizable audience, first on local stations and then on the Mutual network.[13]

---

[11]"Preaching to Eight Cities Simultaneously," *Four Square*, Sept. 1924, p. 29.
[12]KFSG fact file, by R. W. Becker (available in the records of Angelus Temple).
[13]"TV Evangelism," *The Wall Street Journal*, Feb. 1, 1971.

SINAI AND THE SPECTACULAR

Rex Humbard grew up during the depression. Frequently, they "said grace for food they didn't have," but somehow there was money for mandolins for the girls, a guitar for Rex, and a banjo for his brother. Despite his fame today, Humbard remembers his days of traveling evangelism very well. At 13 he saw the Ringling Brothers Circus come to town. The spectacle of the big top going up transfixed the young evangelist. He thought, "If God had a tent like that, he'd have a crowd like that. God ought to be on Main Street where anyone can find Him."[14] Forty years later, the five-thousand-seat Cathedral of Tomorrow is a majestic temple of steel, stone, and style, but it is easy to see that it is really the ultimate gospel big-top.

In 1942 Rex married Maude Aimee Jones (her middle name was in honor of Mrs. McPherson) at Cadle Tabernacle in Indianapolis with 8500 in the audience. Since then the two have worked together in Christian ministry. Maude Aimee is the main musical attraction and Rex the preacher.[15]

The response his father received during a tent crusade in Akron in 1952 led Rex to leave the family troupe and—with $65.00 in his pocket—launch a ministry of his own in an old theater. He called it Calvary Temple. The crowds flocked in, and the congregation grew apace. Soon it was necessary to hold five services each Sunday. Humbard turned first to radio to reach the growing masses, but soon came to recognize an even more potent medium: television was "a God-given miracle for reaching countless millions of unsaved persons with the saving message of Jesus Christ."[16]

> I saw this new thing called television and I said, "That's it." God had given us that thing ... the most powerful force of communication, to take the gospel into the homes. ... We are going to use this thing called television to take a simple church service into every state in the union. That's our number one goal, our number one purpose for having a church and for living.[17]

[14]*Ibid.*
[15]*Time*, May 17, 1971.
[16]*The Answer*, July-Aug. 1972, p. 10.
[17]Personal interview with the author.

MODELS OF RELIGIOUS BROADCASTING

But not everyone shared Humbard's vision. The stations were uninterested and the people looked on television as the "sin box." It required sixteen years of pleading and praying and working to achieve a modest network of 68 stations. But the idea had finally caught on. Rex Humbard was the "undisputed king of television preachers."[18] His ratings went up, and stations began calling him and asking to air the show.

The next year the number of stations rose to 110; the two following years brought an additional hundred stations a year. His TV empire included all of North America. In some urban centers the Humbard television ministry is carried by as many as five channels.

> No single program in the history of television has been given such exposure and few preachers in this country have enjoyed a following such as Humbard's. At present his weekly audience equals in number the total population of Canada and as long as he can continue to pay for his extensive air time—it will cost him just under $7,000,000 this year—it will continue to grow.[19]

Despite serious setbacks in his ministry that were unrelated to the telecast, the old-time religion had become big business for Humbard—at a time when church attendance is generally declining. The sustained spectacular growth is unquestionably owed to the quality of the television spectacle Humbard produces weekly at Cathedral of Tomorrow.

Humbard senses more hunger for simple religion today than ever before. People want to be told how to live. His response to the need he perceives is to entertain, soothe, and seduce his audience with good theater in drama and song while he prepares to hammer home a simple moral or theological point. His performance is never drudgery. It is a joy to observe whether or not one is hearing what he is saying. "He is a great entertainer—in the best sense; he knows television and knows how to utilize it."[20]

The Humbard broadcasts originate directly from the

---

[18]Robert Douglas, "How TV's Top Preacher Built a $14 Million Empire," *Toronto Daily Star*, May 1, 1971.
[19]*Ibid.*
[20]Personal conversation with Donald Stockford of the Cleveland Council of Churches.

church platform. The experience provided the television audience is the regular worship service. The environment is bound to impress the viewer. As described by *The Wall Street Journal*,

> The cathedral is a domed, round, two-story building made of marble and glass that almost any city would be glad to have as a municipal auditorium. It has a huge electronic pipe organ with three sets of pipes. Sitting in the auditorium, you might almost feel you're watching the Ed Sullivan show—except for the 100-foot-long illuminated cross overhead. The cross has 5,000 bulbs that can change colors from white to red to blue or provide various color combinations.[21]

During the service Humbard concentrates on personal moralism and avoids contemporary issues of social morality. He tailors his presentation to the television audience. The rationale for avoiding controversial subjects is simple: "I am neither a general nor a politician," he says. "For me to preach about the Vietnam war would be like going to the blacksmith to get a tooth pulled." The rationale may be simple, but the technique is sophisticated television.

A typical one-hour Humbard program begins with Mrs. Humbard singing a few gospel songs to get things rolling. Duets, trios, and massed choirs of fifty to a hundred voices vary the musical fare and offer a variety of spectacular shots for the cameramen. The view on the screen switches to members of the congregation—praying, singing, laughing, weeping. The musical variety show lasts about half an hour, punctuated by an occasional homiletic jab from Humbard. (Sample fare: "We ought to love sinners. There is not a man or woman in this audience that Jesus does not love.")

Rex Humbard, Jr., directs the television show. From the control booth he fires crisp orders at the cameramen. "Camera one, catch the tear on the blonde, front left. Number two, see what you can pick up on the right. Camera four, hold the cover shot of the girls' trio. Camera three, zoom in on the preacher."

The television spectacle rolls on to the sermon—always short. The mood turns serious as Humbard begins . . . "If

---

[21]"TV Evangelism," *The Wall Street Journal*, Feb. 1, 1971.

your heart quit beating today, how many could say they have the peace of God in their soul?" The grammar doesn't matter: hands go up all over the audience. The cameras dive in for an old man here, a demure young lady there, a mother with small children. At the end of the sermon Humbard calls the people to the altar for confession and dedication. He anoints them there—oil on the forehead. Rex, Jr., yells at his cameraman, "Grab me a good anointing." Humbard invites the home audience to kneel and join in prayer. The camera catches tearful faces, bowed heads, writhing fingers, an old lady mumbling away her sin.

Then Maude Aimee is back. Her solos are the most popular. Sometimes her husband grabs a guitar and strums along. Her brother, the Rev. Wayne Jones, wraps up the television program from a separate studio, while Humbard puts the finishing touches on the worship service in the Cathedral, including counseling after the altar call.

Humbard periodically cements the allegiance of his massive following with TV rallies held throughout the country. He packs the core of the 150-member cathedral staff into his four-engine Vickers-Viscount and flies to a distant city, always returning to Akron for his Sunday show. The televised rally incorporates many elements of the Sunday show. Television starlets march on stage in bright dresses singing songs like "Put Your Hand in the Hand of the Man from Galilee." The music ranges over Gospel to Blues to slightly jazzy. Humbard may play his guitar; he will surely preach. The message will be like those heard in the cathedral on Sunday.

It takes more than simplicity, style, and spectacle to keep Humbard's spectacle together. The Cathedral budget of a half million a year is raised by that local congregation; the television budget, which approaches $10 million a year, is raised by listener contributions. The Cathedral of Tomorrow, Inc., a nonprofit organization, owns three commercial enterprises that generate resources for the total ministry—Real Form Girdle, Unity Electronics, and an advertising agency. There is no question that Rex Humbard is big business. His broadcast follow-up ministry is computerized, and every letter received from a viewer is answered with a specially tailored reply which solicits

SINAI AND THE SPECTACULAR

funds to continue the ministry. Nearly two million people read Humbard's printed messages in his magazine, *The Answer*, copies of his sermons, special brochures, and personalized letters.

Computers also continually evaluate each station that carries the program. Each is expected to generate enough viewer mail to provide the contributions needed to pay for its own air time. Stations failing to generate the requisite financial returns are dropped.

Humbard thinks of himself as an evangelical, not a fundamentalist. He thinks fundamentalists are too often negative in their emphasis. The evangelical wants to be positive. He wants to "get out and reach people, whether it's feeding someone who is hungry or clothing someone who is naked or praying for someone who's sinned. I preach a little hell-fire . . . but you're not going to *scare* people. . . . No, you're going to take people a lot further with love and compassion."[22] What he is doing, he feels, is what the mainline churches were doing a generation ago—staying with the fundamentals.

There is a danger in Humbard's flamboyant style—a danger of which he is well aware. The three great temptations are pride, greed, and sex. But if he can keep his finances straight in this day and age, his ministry may continue to grow for a long time and his "professional blend of folksy, pep-talk piety and bubbly inspirational hill-billy music—a Norman Vincent Peale to a Lawrence Welk constituency" continue to swell the numbers of dollars and people.[23]

Humbard addresses the individual, not the world. The solution to broad social problems will only come through persons changed around in terms of Christ's way. "If I get enough people in the United States and Canada to pray, we could get a million people to come to church and become Christians. If all those people feed the hungry, we'd solve a lot of problems."[24] As for the Vietnam War,

---

[22] Clifford Terry, "It's a Far Cry from the Church in the Wildwood," *TV Guide*, Sept. 12, 1972.

[23] *Time*, May 17, 1971.

[24] John Dart, "Evangelist Parlays TV Into Massive Following," *Los Angeles Times*, Jan. 30, 1972.

Time says, Humbard's response was hesitant: "I dunno. Before I'd say anything about Vietnam I'd have to hear the Lord speak twicet!"[25]

What God does speak to Humbard, he in turn speaks to 20,000,000 around the world. When Humbard arrives on stage, God's weekly invasion is well underway. It is Sinai all over again—a new Sinai every seven days. Only fifteen minutes of it is sermon, but there is an hour of scintillating spectacle which says "God is awesome! God is glorious! God can be gracious! Fear and tremble, saints and sinners! Christ is the answer!"

"The play's the thing" for Rex Humbard—and he plays his Sinai spectacularly!

Oral Roberts

When Oral Roberts produces a broadcast spectacular he is merely re-enacting the form of God's dealings with man, as he sees them. Miracles and supernatural intervention and mighty acts of God have played an important role in the career of this well-known contemporary follower of the frontier Methodists and Jonathan Edwards.

Roberts was born on January 24, 1918, in Pontotac County, Oklahoma. The address was rural, the culture a barren quest for survival. His father, Ellis Roberts, was an evangelist in the Pilgrim Holiness Church, having broken with the Methodists because of their lack of appreciation for his experience and proclamation of the charismatic gift of speaking in tongues. His inclination to exhort and testify of his beliefs led him to the role of Pentecostal evangelist.

His father's chosen vocation had a tremendous effect on the life of his son. His theological stance is preserved in Oral Roberts' confessional outlook. The psychological characteristics of the Pentecostal evangelist shape Roberts' view of what religious experience is and what one is to look for in true Christianity. The grinding poverty of his early life—sometimes near starvation—haunts Oral Roberts today as he pursues his ministry of delivering the world from its suffering of body, mind, and soul.

[25]*Time*, May 17, 1971.

SINAI AND THE SPECTACULAR

By his early teens, Roberts had had all he could take of Pentecostal fervor and famine. He made plans to leave home. His parents protested and told him that he would never be able to go farther than their prayers. Roberts walked out of the house anyway, never intending to return. He went to Atoka, Oklahoma, and a job with a judge. As handyman for the judge's home, grocery clerk, newsboy, reporter for the *Ada Evening News*, high school honor student, basketball player, and class president he soon worked himself into a physical collapse. The basketball coach picked him up, unconscious, off the gymnasium floor. His lungs were riddled with the dreaded tuberculosis. He returned home—not in the way his praying parents had in mind, but home nonetheless.

Oral saw the event as disaster. "I was heading back to poverty, back to a religion I had never accepted, back to my parents' discipline, and it tore me up inside."[26] No medical treatment was available for tuberculosis, and he lay near death almost a year. Then one day his sister came in and announced with authority, "Oral, God is going to heal you." It awakened him from his depression and semicoma. His brother Elmer soon reinforced the hope of health by announcing, "Oral, get up. God is going to heal you." The family carried Oral to an evangelist's crusade.

> I suddenly knew God was going to heal me. . . . God spoke to my heart promising to heal me and He called me to take His healing power to my generation. His words rang clear to me: "Son, I am going to heal you and you are to take the message of my healing power to your generation."
>
> Though I didn't have any idea what that meant, I did know that now my life was in His hands. I have never ceased to believe it.
>
> When we arrived at the tent, they put me in a rocking chair with pillows on both sides, and when the evangelist finished preaching, they carried me up to him. He put his hands on my head and said a short prayer, "Thou foul disease! I command you in the name of Jesus Christ to come out of this boy's lungs. Loose him and let him go!"
>
> The next thing I knew I was racing back and forth on the platform shouting at the top of my voice, "I am healed! I am healed! I am healed!"[27]

---

[26] Roberts, *The Call: An Autobiography*, p. 26.
[27] *Ibid.*, p. 34.

MODELS OF RELIGIOUS BROADCASTING

At a clinic in Ada shortly thereafter, a fluoroscopy indicated healthy lungs. The miracle made him a minister of miracles. Two months later he began his preaching career.

Roberts attended Oklahoma Baptist University and Phillips University. He evangelized and pastored churches in the Pilgrim Holiness Church for twelve years after his healing. In 1947 he arrived in Enid, Oklahoma, and it was there, he feels, that his "real ministry" began.

Since his healing he had felt a persistent restlessness. Pastoral work and evangelism left him frustrated and dissatisfied, as though none of it really mattered.[28] The suffering people around him seldom looked to the church for help. His associates urged him to settle down, but he could not:

> I was dying on the vine. Each week began to be more and more of a struggle. How could I get up and preach about Jesus making the lame to walk, the dumb to talk, the deaf to hear, the blind to see, the leper to be cleansed, and the dead raised to life and then let it all be treated as something in the past, something irrelevant to our life and time? How could I talk about the Bible being in the *now?*
>
> I began to be consumed with a passion either to have a ministry like Jesus or to get out of the ministry.[29]

Under that emotional and spiritual duress he began to have a recurring dream, which he believes God sent as a way of "dealing mightily" with him. It was a haunting vision of humanity "lost, sick, afraid, frustrated, tormented, oppressed.... I heard their screams of fear and misery, their sobs, their wails of frustration. What I saw and heard tore me to pieces."[30]

In a sociology class at Phillips University Roberts was disturbed by the "unbiblical scientism" of his professor. He considered his reaction to be a "call of God" to truth that heals. This was his second experience of special divine revelation.

---

[28] Oral Roberts, *My Twenty Years of a Miracle Ministry*, p. 7.
[29] Roberts, *The Call*, pp. 37f.
[30] Roberts, *My Twenty Years*, p. 8.

SINAI AND THE SPECTACULAR

> Suddenly from out of my spirit I heard God's voice again, *Son, don't be like other men. Don't be like other preachers. Be like my Son Jesus and heal the people as He healed them....* God showed me there was only one source of original information about Jesus and that is the Bible. He impressed me to read the Gospels and Acts through three times during the next thirty days.[31]

He submerged himself in the first five books of the New Testament. He read them all on his knees in the fashion of the most austere monastic ritual. He fasted and prayed. Often he found himself weeping and overwrought with strange and inexplicable emotion. Frequently he felt as though Jesus were in the room with him.

> I achieved a harmony with Jesus while reading the four Gospels and the Book of Acts. What He had done during His earthly ministry and what I felt I should do in my ministry were one and the same—to preach the Gospel and to heal the sick. I wanted my ministry to be against the same four things His was against—sin, demons, disease and fear. I wanted my ministry to emphasize the same power that His did—the miracle-working power of faith in God.[32]

He was certain he could not minister like Jesus without a direct contact from God. Lying flat on the floor of his study, emotionally distraught and exhausted, he heard God speak to him. Still, he set up three conditions God had to meet to prove he had truly spoken: he wanted a thousand people at his evangelistic crusade in Enid the following Sunday, funds for the crusade, and divine healing of the people so conclusive that they would recognize his calling. The three conditions were met: the audience was 1200; the offering was $3.03 more than costs; and people were healed. Roberts' illumination on the floor of his little church was verified:

> I saw that God was good, that it was His will to heal and make whole, and that He was the source of abundant life. He spoke to me and left me without any doubt that He had called me to take His healing power to my generation. I was ready to take the steps to enter world evangelism through a ministry of healing.[33]

---

[31]*Ibid.*
[32]*Ibid.*
[33]Roberts, *The Call,* p. 40.

In the twenty-seven years since his illumination Roberts has written several books, preached to every inhabited continent, edited a monthly magazine, built a university, ministered on two weekly nationally televised programs aired to every state and province of the USA and Canada over 325 stations, and reportedly healed thousands of the people he has addressed. All this grew out of the extra $3.03 the twelve hundred people gave, "but more than that, by the God of Heaven who chose to raise up a ministry to recapture for the church the healing of Jesus."

Roberts is a supernaturalist. He believes that God operates in life and history by miraculous events. Most of us most of the time are not sensitive to these supernatural acts of God, Dr. Roberts admits. God is, nonetheless, invading our world and intervening in our affairs regularly. He does not simply act through natural causes. He works supernaturally in our lives.

His own life testifies to this, he believes. His deliverance from death of tuberculosis was a miracle. The revelation by which God called him to take divine healing to the masses was a miracle. God's appearance to him in Enid to call him to crusade for Christ was a miracle. The confirmation of that call was a miracle. The opportunity to take his ministry to every continent, the growth of the Oral Roberts Association, the rise and rapid accreditation of Oral Roberts University, the development of his nationally televised programs were all miracles.

Roberts feels that there is a great desire for the miraculous boiling to the surface in this generation. People feel and see futility everywhere, in government, in science, in militarism, in urban sprawl, in churches, in religious life. Roberts believes that most humans today share his gripping conviction that "without a miracle from God we have nothing." People everywhere "desire . . . the miracle power of Christ." So the visitor to Oral Roberts University in Tulsa will see numerous signs around the campus, confronting passersby with a supernaturalist view of life. "Expect a miracle" the signs read. For Roberts and his university students, miracles are a reality . . . a necessity.

Since the secret of life is in expecting miracles, it is not surprising that Roberts' television and radio ministries are designed with the spectacle format. Each show is intended to bring to the international audience a "mighty act of God."

It was a natural transition for Roberts to move from tent crusades to radio to television. The international scope of the latter is not surprising in view of the international scope of the former. From his entry into crusade evangelism in 1947 he has taken the whole world as his parish. By 1953 he was holding fourteen crusades a year in major American population centers, each crusade centering around the miracle of faith-healing. The gospel music set the stage; the sermon created the "spirit"; the dramatic "laying of hands" was the instrument. And that "mighty act of God" was finally the purpose and objective of Roberts' crusading. At this time Roberts heard God speak again: "*You are to win a million souls in the next 36 months. I staggered and reeled under this command.... How could I do it?*"[34]

Roberts took his tent around the world on "adventures with God." Every nation or continent he visited responded with larger crowds of tormented people than he could accommodate. The public press provided an incessantly open window through which whole countries could witness the drama. But Roberts still felt restless about "all those unreached."

> There were 26 million television sets in the United States and the number was growing every day. It was a new and exciting medium; people were captivated by TV and anxious to watch it. I began to use television as an outreach of my ministry.... Our first television program was premiered on January 10, 1954, over sixteen stations.[35]

The audience response was immediate and overwhelming, but Roberts was dissatisfied with the woodenness of the program. Rex Humbard encouraged Roberts to film directly in the tent to provide the immediate sense of God's acting miraculously before the eye of the camera. The $42,000 required to do that paid off handsomely:

---

[34] Roberts, *My Twenty Years*, p. 25.
[35] *Ibid.*

> The first program filmed direct during the crusade was aired in February, 1955. It created a national controversy. At our office in Tulsa we were flooded with calls, and television stations throughout North America were totally unprepared for the response they received. Their switchboards were jammed; their mail was unprecedented.
>
> It shook some station managers so much that our program was cancelled. Then they really began to get mail. Millions were excited by our program and wanted it shown on their favorite station.[36]

It was especially the march of the penitents and the healings that created the dramatic effect.

Early in his television ministry Roberts was confronted with Anne Williams, an auto accident cripple. Before recovering from the accident Anne was crippled further with polio; then she contracted spondylitis and was a permanent "wheelchair victim." In the living room of a friend while viewing the telecast of the Oral Roberts crusade, Anne got up and walked. The spectacle she observed on television had reached across the miles to become a mighty act of God in her life. This became the most publicized healing of Roberts' ministry and led to a surge of expansion in crusade and mass media ministry.

The format for Roberts' television from 1955 to 1967 was typically the tent crusade setting, whether filmed in the tent or in a studio. The emphasis was upon God's healing invasion of human lives. The technique was that of a divine impact upon the home viewer as he experienced the "miracle of God" unfolding before his eyes on the screen. By 1962 Roberts was beginning to feel that this format was outmoded. Television popularity had shifted from the drama of the early 1950s to fast-moving variety shows. Roberts began to feel the need to leave television if he could not compete with the "new television," which emphasized the spectacular even more than his crusades did. He began to cut out low-response and high-cost stations. In 1965 he decided that he would terminate his television spectaculars by 1967, and in 1966 he cut his station list by half, terminating the rest a year later.

[36]Roberts, *The Call*, p. 180.

SINAI AND THE SPECTACULAR

In September 1967 he went into worldwide radio.[37] English and Spanish broadcasts took him to South America, Africa, and Europe, as well as North America. The format centered in live interviews and on-the-air testimonies about God's miraculous intervention into personal lives. There were sermons and music, but the central thrust was the talks with individuals whom "God has made . . . whole in body, mind, and spirit."

Roberts himself switched to the United Methodist Church in 1968. Subsequently, he felt a "new anointing" in his ministry, and poured great energy into finding the new format for the "television for the seventies." His son Richard, Dick Ross of Billy Graham Films, Ralph Carmichael, and others got together to build a new kind of show. The "Oral Roberts Contact Special" was conceived. The announcer was from "Bonanza," the technical crew from "Laugh-In," the set built by NBC. The result was an even more spectacular spectacle than in the old days. In March 1969 the first Oral Roberts special hit the airways. It covered all of North America. The response was an explosion.

> It created a sensation in the religious field. For a religious group to use the medium of television creatively was a new experience. . . . We had entered the world of secular entertainment and made it serve as a way of getting the attention of the unchurched. The first half of the show got their attention and then kept them with us in the second half as we shared the message God had given us.[38]

Roberts had moved successfully into the "variety show" format. Pat Boone, Anita Bryant, Dale Evans, Jerry Lewis, Jimmy Durante, and Jimmy Rogers helped make the spectacles even more spectacular. Although some traditionalists misunderstood the entertainment orientation, the response exceeded anything Roberts had known in his career as a purveyor of crusade spectaculars. The Thanksgiving special of 1970 reached over 27 million people. Thousands of young people wrote for advice and prayer. What they had

---

[37] Oral Roberts, *My Personal Diary of Our World-wide Ministry*, p. 10.
[38] Roberts, *The Call*, p. 195.

seen had convinced them God was acting miraculously in our time and they wanted access to that power.

But the new spectacle may not be a permanent approach to the masses. Roberts is nothing if not flexible. Of one thing he is convinced: television is here to stay, and it is one of the most effective and exciting ways to reach people where they are.[39] Religious broadcasters have challenged Roberts' new approach as television of the 1960s rather than the 1970s, and argue that there must be a move beyond drama and variety formats to spot-TV and documentaries. Yet Roberts' new format seems to be working well in the 1970s. If the time comes for him to change, only one thing is certain: whatever format he uses in his ministry, the purpose will always be to make God's inbreaking, miraculous presence a meaningful event in the lives of humans hungry for the supernatural. Roberts will always be spectacular.

Billy Graham

Asked why he would not sell broadcast time to a denomination, but would sell it to Billy Graham, a CBS network official once replied, "Billy Graham is a national institution."

Graham has been an American institution for many years. As advisor to five presidents and conscience-keeper of the citizenry, he stands for American moralism—indeed, he has largely shaped it.

Surely one secret of his success is that he has kept apace of events. Born four days before the trench warfare in Flanders Field was finished by the November armistice, he is still striding with youthful vigor as the automated air war in Indochina ebbs and flows. He has managed to be contemporary, perhaps even *avant-garde* in his ministry, though he reaches from rural origins to international sophistication, from coal stoves to energy crises, from "stump-preaching" to mass media. He is always up-to-date in his technology and techniques, and, he insists, always "old-fashioned" in his gospel, which is rooted in historic biblical Christianity.

---

[39]*Ibid.*, p. 196.

SINAI AND THE SPECTACULAR

Graham's career began with speaking engagements at Youth-for-Christ rallies and local evangelism missions. A skilled and talented speaker, the Wheaton graduate came quickly to the attention of the leaders of American evangelicalism. His missionary zeal led him to consider work in Tibet, China, and South America, but no clear "divine leading" came for any one of them. He traveled to England for a clearer view of the work of overseas mission societies and of human need.

Wherever Graham went he was remembered for his bluntly direct assessments of human suffering against the backdrop of that which is tragic in society. Physical and social suffering apparently tormented him as well as emotional and spiritual evil. In 1948 and 1949 the ministry of crusade evangelism began, but early efforts in Modesto and Los Angeles were not strikingly successful, and one in Altoona, Pennsylvania, was a "flop."[40] Graham did not give up, and in the Fall of 1949 success set in. Cowboy star Stuart Hamblin and gangster Jim Vaus were converted at a Los Angeles tent crusade. The press was enthusiastic. The campaign extended from the planned three weeks to eight.

After Los Angeles the ministry caught fire. Across the country Graham held crusades, and his reputation picked up strength. Then Walter A. Maier of "The Lutheran Hour" suddenly died.

> Dr. Maier had had the ear of America, preaching a clear evangelical Gospel in the context of the social, political and moral state of the nation. Billy and the Team immediately prayed together that someone be raised to take Maier's place.[41]

Many churchmen saw Graham himself as the heir to Maier's radio popularity, but he was not easily convinced. Weekly broadcasts, he feared, would be a full-time job that would obstruct his crusading. At the crusade in Portland, Oregon, he decided to "put out the fleece" and test God's will, challenging him to send $25,000 by midnight. The offering that came in was only $23,500. Graham declared it was the devil who had sent it to tempt him. If God wanted him in radio, he would have sent all the

---

[40] John Pollock, *Billy Graham: The Authorized Biography*, p. 51.
[41] *Ibid.*, pp. 79f.

money needed. But when he returned to his hotel $1500 in special sealed envelopes awaited him. God had supernaturally intervened.

What Billy had learned in crusading he carried to the broadcast "Hour of Decision." Stirring music, vivid biblicism, colorful damnation of evil, concrete illustration, confrontation of the timid, anxious, guilt-ridden, and insecure, and the spectacular climax of the altar call—these were the ingredients of the tent meeting, the radio broadcast, and, from 1955 on, of his television ministry.

On Good Friday 1955 Billy Graham was at Kelvin Hall in Glasgow. His crusade was telecast by BBC directly from the hall. The spectacle of fiery prophet, mass response, marching penitents, and moving music came alive before the eyes of the viewing audience. The impact was an explosive surprise to the Graham team. The evangelist who had stirred whole cities but restlessly looked for a larger role had finally found his real arena—the telecast crusade. From Kelvin Hall Graham took the idea to Madison Square Garden on June 1, 1955, "and each following Saturday (seventeen in all) was a revelation to America."[42]

> The very fact that the pictures emanated from the country's best known arena made them doubly impressive. As a television ministry it was a thousand times more effective than the Graham team's studio program of earlier years, for the crowd in the Garden created a strong sense of participation for the viewer, who was not eavesdropping an event, not watching a contrived half hour of song and talk.[43]

Graham had hit his stride and found his strategy: the religious spectacle.

The Sinai spectacular saves souls for Graham as well as for Roberts and Humbard. Much of Graham's broadcasting since 1955 has been in the form of telecast crusades. He buys most of his air time on both radio and television. He can get prime time frequently and network time when he wants it, but he does not need either to reach millions. After nearly twenty spectacularly successful years, his audience will come to him on radio and television regardless of station or time of day.

[42]*Ibid.*, p. 180.
[43]*Ibid.*

Graham supports his broadcasts with a massive literature follow-up. The "Hour of Decision" is reinforced by *Decision* magazine, the largest-circulation religious magazine in the United States. It is a substantive—sometimes almost scholarly—*slick* periodical. Graham's syndicated newspaper column "My Answer" is as well known as Ann Landers. The counseling service provided by Graham's crusade team, together with the cooperative organization of local churches, is an important part of Graham's ministry.

But the center of it all is the spectacle, God's mighty act in Billy Graham's arena before the eyes of the whole world. It is Graham's way of confessing that for him, God is miracle, God is supernatural, God invades his world explosively to redeem it. Its success has made Graham a twentieth-century American religious institution with an Old Testament trademark.

The Divine Invasion

There are many other less well-known examples of the "Sinai syndrome" in religious broadcasting. Good men and bad have used this technique. The spectacle broadcasters have varied in character from honorable Christians burdened for souls to disreputable shysters, from personality cultists and megalomaniacs to earnest pastors and honest humanists.

Howard and Sarah Kernochan's 1972 documentary film *Marjoe* depicts in lurid detail how a disreputable fake can exploit people with the religious spectacle. The film is Marjoe Gortner's story of "how he hustled the word of the Lord" and turned his spiritual vaudeville act into a large personal fortune. Marjoe started plying his religious trade at the age of four. He ranged the Bible Belt with great success for a generation. At twenty-eight he "abandoned evangelism with a vengeance," filmed *Marjoe* for self-publicity, and is waiting for Hollywood to make him a famous actor.

Television crusades have not been free of the Marjoe type. Still, the "personality cult" in broadcasting is not necessarily dishonest or undesirable. Certainly Aimee Semple McPherson developed a personality cult, as have Humbard, Roberts, and Graham. An element of the success of each is the amplification of his personality through the exposure the evangelistic crusade and religious broadcasting provide. But all these were people of superior personality potential before they got the exposure. If they had not been, they would not have succeeded in developing the organizations necessary to achieve and support the exposure.

One may justly criticize each of these figures on numerous counts—after all, they are all human. But the focus on personality is in itself potentially as wholesome and necessary for effective communication of the gospel as it is *potentially* unwholesome and exploitative.

The major criticism of the "Sinai syndrome" in religious broadcasting must be a theological one. The religious broadcasting spectacle operates with the same limited view of the nature and behavior of God that Jesus opposed in Judaism, the view of Old Testament supernaturalism rather than New Testament incarnation.

All the evangelists of the spectacle operate with the restrictive assumption that God functions in supernatural rather than natural ways in the healing and guidance that Christianity calls salvation. Their view of God is thus one of someone so transcendent that he must explosively invade his world and our lives in order to function in them. God's presence and behavior become "unnatural" to life and to man.

Such a view is an erroneous Old Testament one. It sees God's presence not in incarnation but in mysterious forces which are especially at play in disturbances of history or of personal lives. The divine disturbances are often of a detrimental nature until they succeed in breaking a man and he turns to God. Such forces and their disturbances are to be seen in the traumatic spectacles of the Exodus from Egypt, Sinai, the conquest of Canaan, the fall of the kingdom, the Babylonian captivity, and—today—in the televised crusades. God invades in each case. The event is "the Day of the Lord" of the Old Testament prophets. It is a moment of judgment and salvation by God himself. The Graham broadcast is, therefore, "The Hour of Decision." "Multitudes, multitudes" of television viewers are standing "in the valley of decision" (Joel 3:14).

SINAI AND THE SPECTACULAR

If Jesus is the clue to essential Christianity, that Old Testament view of God is wrong and its perpetration in the television spectacle less than wholesome for healthy human spirituality. Jesus represented God as present in his world in grace, not judgment, as a healer not a threat, "in the form of a servant," not crashing through in a spectacle. Jesus does not represent mysterious forces of an awesome nature, which supernaturally keep men on tenterhooks until the explosive moment of revelation. He represents a natural life-style within the world frame where God lives through the Holy Spirit in the spirit of stable, healthy humans. He is the God of growing minds and relationships, developing attitudes and honesty.

It is only human to prefer being impressed to being loved. We are more inclined to accept a romantic or dramatic fiction than to face up to reality. The authenticity required by being loved makes us vulnerable. Thus we are disinclined to desire that religious and spiritual reality which demands our being real and whole persons. We are more naturally inclined to that religious performance which impresses us with its spectacular character.

The individuals who make up the worldwide television audience can experience such impressiveness when viewing a spectacular. In experiencing it they can identify with the charisma and personality of the world-famous evangelist, reinforcing their own ego, gaining a sense of admirable identity, suggesting partnership in massive and divine things far beyond their own often paltry lives. Even further identification with the spectacle can come from sending money and receiving literature.

Too easily the Sinai spectacle becomes a manipulative exploitation of human anxiety and gullibility. It substitutes inauthentic ego-reinforcement for authentic spiritual growth. To that extent it is a dangerous enterprise.

This is not to criticize everything Graham, Humbard, Roberts, McPherson, and others of this type have done. It is merely to call attention to the built-in obstructions their technique raises to spiritual maturity. Never to go beyond the representation of God as the transcendent intervener is to foster an un-Christian spirituality rooted in false expectations. The Christian ministry, to be authentic, must

MODELS OF RELIGIOUS BROADCASTING

represent God *as he is in Christ*—incarnate, emptied of his spectacular divinity (Phil. 2), dwelling as a man with men, functioning as a servant, natural, unspectacular, virtually unobtrusive; healing by forgiveness, relief, maturity, and trust. A technique of ministry must be found—even in broadcasting—which implies an image or model of God shaped like Jesus of Nazareth.

The Sinai spectacle inevitably leads down a dead-end street to a spiritual substitute for the simple, substantive love of God. The spectacle implies a low view of man as one who is brought to redemption by being taken in by the Madison Avenue techniques of an evangelism that sells him what he needs whether he wants it or not.

five
Electronic Education

Jesus was often called "Teacher," apparently reflecting the impact he had on those around him. What he said and how he lived brought new insights to his peers, lessons and insights that changed their lives.

There is in Christian tradition a sturdy strand that conceives of Christianity as a redemptive influence in human life mainly in terms of its power to teach the truth. A continuous company of great churchmen representing that tradition stretches across Christian history. These teachers of the faith, with their tradition of healing through insight, do not stand opposed to the idea that Christianity is a "life to be lived." But their technique as great thinkers and teachers stands in contrast to the methodology of those who envision Christianity as "redemption by emotional crisis" (as we saw in the previous discussion of the Sinai spectacle) and those who see Christianity as salvation by divine visitation (as in the current charismatic movement).

MODELS OF RELIGIOUS BROADCASTING

Not surprisingly, there are some religious broadcasters who identify with that tradition emphasizing "healing by insight" and growth through learning. They believe the church should use radio and television to teach. They see the camera and microphone as an extension of the lecture hall podium. They insist that broadcasting facilities are tools to be used in the struggle with ideas and the insight and growth it brings.

The model for this type of religious broadcast is that of the rabbi, the teacher of Judaism. The rabbinic model entails two crucial Christian concepts—a gracious view of God and a high view of man.

God is seen to function in his world in a natural and immanent way. He is present not as a stranger and a threat, but as friend, teacher, and Savior. The rabbinic model is essentially the "incarnation" concept. God entered his world in human form for healing purposes. He heals through the expanded and corrected grasp of reality and truth that can be achieved by humans with the aid of the divinely led teacher. Man is thus seen as a child of God who can grasp reality and truth through his native emotional, intellectual, and spiritual faculties, provided they are stimulated and directed by the "revealer," the teacher. Camera and microphone can be employed to foster the encounter between a Christian teacher and the human multitudes.

The assumption is that the presence of God's Spirit and word in a wise and mature Christian is a kind of "incarnation," which can project itself to humanity through teaching the Christian way by clear and wise insights. Humans, in turn, can digest such insights to their great spiritual, intellectual, and moral growth, by means of the dynamics and abilities of man's own nature.

The model of an "incarnate God" is certainly a New Testament concept. The model of a rational, intelligent, inquiring human, capable of redemption through understanding and commitment, is a sound Greek-Christian idea, surely consonant with the church fathers, likely with Paul, and not inconsistent with the rabbinic role of Jesus of Nazareth.

The pedagogical model of the rabbi has the virtue of

representing God as a present friend who interacts with humans through Christian persons. In that interaction he cajoles people into focusing on the real questions of life and meaning, at the same time suggesting the kinds of answers that soundly suit those questions. God is, in this view, supportive of man, gracious to limited and inadequate persons, relating for the purpose of healing, not damning.

Many broadcasters might be listed as illustrations of this model in religious radio and television. M. R. De Haan for many years aired a broadcast that he called "The Radio Bible Class." The program was limited to radio, was essentially a series of lectures on Scripture, and frequently fell into a homiletic style and theological speculation of the most imaginative sort. De Haan's intent, however, was to teach through radio. His son Richard currently conducts the weekly broadcast for an apparently nationwide audience. Though its content and techniques are limited, "The Radio Bible Class" is a podium on radio. The program minimizes mood-setting music and staging, lead-in, and introductions, and it maximizes the lecture-homily teaching of Christian ideas and theological concepts. It is thus typical of a multitude of local and national religious broadcasts.

In a sense even Aimee Semple McPherson sometimes used the religious broadcast as an extension of the podium. She is best remembered for her mastery of the spectacle format, but she also lectured regularly on radio, and her midweek and Sunday evening programs often took the teaching format.

Presbyterian Church, US

In some cases, then, it is difficult to distinguish absolutely between the pulpit format and the podium style. But the broadcast ministries of the late Dr. John Alexander of the Presbyterian Church in the United States (Southern) and of Professor Roger L. Shinn of Union Theological Seminary are clearly in the realm of pedagogy.

It was Alexander who focused for the Southern Presbyterians the idea that religious broadcasting should be a teaching ministry. As a Presbyterian pastor experienced in local radio broadcasting, he urged a denominational broadcast ministry in 1944. He was instrumental in the establishment of the Southern Religious Radio Commission and the Protestant Radio and Television Center in Atlanta. In 1953 television productions by the Presbyterians were underway. By 1958 the denomination had created TRAV, an agency for ministry through television, radio and audio-visual techniques.

The Presbyterians' broadcasting mandate, as stated by the General Assembly, is

> to use effectively Television... to reach for Christ those yet unreached; to add a new dimension to the Christian experience of those who are already believers, for the purpose of further enlightening, inspiring, and activating them; to undergird and strengthen through the newly reached and newly inspired, the work of the local church; to portray to the world the truths of the gospel of Christ as they apply to the world in which we live.[1]

The early television productions of the denomination were spots of a minute or less, intended as supplements to brief meditations on television. This was a technique long used on radio. In 1955 the Presbyterians began to air a series called "Layman's Witness." These were fifteen-minute film programs, featuring interviews and discussions designed to teach specifically Christian concepts about God and personal religious practice. The late Dr. L. Nelson Bell, missionary to China, was featured, as were Bobby Dodd, football coach at Georgia Tech, Patsy Turner, minister to Appalachia long before that became a popular kind of ministry, and a long list of Christian leaders in American society.

In 1956 an eight-program series by Dr. N. S. Boyles and Dr. W. Elliot, Jr., called "Put God First," was produced as a ministry of evangelism by pedagogy. A thirteen-program series entitled "Man to Man" featured Dr. J. A. Redhead,

---

[1]Promotional brochure entitled "Assembly's Committee on Television, Radio, and Audio Visuals." See also the "Manual for TRAV," Article II, into which the purpose statement is formally incorporated and in which it is amplified.

lecturing on the biblical claims for a Christian life-style. This series received national exposure with the aid of the Broadcasting and Film Commission of the National Council of Churches.

Alexander's influence survived his death in 1958, though a major cooperative film series of thirteen dramas to be made with the United Presbyterian Church in the USA had to be dropped in 1960 before the series could be produced. Economic limitations have cut back Southern Presbyterian broadcasting to spots, but the conviction that successful evangelism in religious broadcasting requires teaching continues; and there is a strong feeling that the spot cannot teach as effectively as the church must. A spokesman for Southern Presbyterian broadcasting, Bluford B. Hestir, has pointed to the critical limitation of the spot: "We cannot teach a course in theology in sixty seconds."[2]

In 1962 TRAV cooperated with WUNC of the University of North Carolina to produce a seventeen-program instructional series called "Biblical Perspectives." Under the direction of Bernard Boyd, the programs discussed such titles as "What does the Bible Really Say?", "The Biblical View of History," "The Bible's Moral Imperative," "The Human Predicament," "Biblical Eschatology—Christian Apocalyptic." In 1963 and 1965 the denomination produced thirty-minute black-and-white tapes for Christmas and Easter. Both followed the teaching format, asking and answering "What is Christmas?" and "What is Easter?" Music was used in a fairly traditional fashion, and the content was predictable. The videotapes continue in use, but they have never achieved any significant national stature.

No doubt TRAV's most renowned effort is "Come Blow Your Horn," a thirty-minute film study of jazz and the church. The filming was done in the studios of WBT in Charlotte, North Carolina, one of the best-equipped in the country. Total production cost was $7,000. The superb talent used in "Come Blow Your Horn" virtually guaranteed success. Director Don McDaniel had produced several

[2]Personal interview with the author.

award-winning shows. The director of music was Loonis McGlohon, who was once Judy Garland's accompanist. He organized a jazz orchestra and, with Hollywood musician Alex Wilder, wrote the music for the special. Marlena Shaw, a soloist for Count Basie, sang. Bob Raiford, a leading Washington radio and television personality and jazz expert, was the narrator.

The show was a great success, and is now syndicated privately by TRAV and distributed through the Educational Television Program Services of Bloomington, Indiana. It had, in effect, educational network distribution, the first denominational program to enjoy that. In general, Southern Presbyterian programming has been distributed by private syndication, more often directly through stations than through local councils of churches. As a result of the popularity of some of its programming, use has been requested by the commercial networks. National television productions of the denomination appear on public service time exclusively.

What John Alexander began in the early 1940s over the radio still lives—the ambition to create broadcast ministries which will *teach* Reformed theology in a way that influences the character of human life.

United Church of Christ

Roger Shinn was Professor of Applied Christianity at Union Theological Seminary in 1965 when Everett C. Parker of the United Church of Christ Office of Communication persuaded him to put his applied Christianity on television. The resultant 13-program, half-hour series—"Tangled World"—turned out to be significant in its message and successful in reaching a wide audience. It was released through private syndication on public service time in 1968. In Pittsburgh alone eight hundred groups met regularly to watch the program and discuss it.

The format of "Tangled World" was documentary. In Shinn's discussion of poverty and affluence the camera moved up Park Avenue in Manhattan through the affluent and slum areas of the avenue. On the way, the viewer passes a lot of churches, some very rich, others obviously

ELECTRONIC EDUCATION

poor. The goal was to stimulate informed discussion about issues that face all humans and must be taken seriously by Christians especially. Such questions as living a life of Christian discipleship in an anonymous, urban society, decision-making, genetic manipulation, and other issues raised by rapid scientific advance were faced head-on. Affluence and poverty gave rise to some of the most dramatic shows of the series. Shooting from a swaying helicopter, the camera exposed the vivid contrasts of the human condition in the nation's largest city. "The important thing is to avoid any retreat from our tangled world," said Shinn in summarizing his course in Christian ethics.[3]

"Tangled World" was clearly intended as a teaching instrument, not as a homily. A book of the same title, containing essentially the text of the series, was published by Scribners in 1965 and distributed with a study guide, and used intensively by the local study groups that sprang up around the television series. Many educational institutions adopted the book as a course textbook, and thousands of Americans still buy it for general reading. In a sense, the profits from the book came too late. Limited finances when the filming was undertaken restricted the series to thirteen black-and-white films, which made the program less attractive than if it had been shot in color.

Parker's motivation for teaching by television is clear and hard-hitting:

> The need was for a program on ethics for adults. We have done a lot for children, over the years. There has never been a program on the air in ethics for adults. In that sense the motivation was theological. I would do it again if we could. I would keep a program on ethics on. I would like to do one on the ethics of power. We had one show in "Tangled World" on politics but you could do a whole series on that.

The lure and agony of the city, racism and its misuse of people, laws and justice, sex, faith and anxiety, the problem of a unified world were all treated in detailed dramatic illustration. It was as though Roger Shinn stood at his podium in Union Theological Seminary in New York and opened the doors of his classroom to 200,000,000 Americans. It was stunningly effective.

[3] Roger Shinn, "Tangled World Discussion Guide."

MODELS OF RELIGIOUS BROADCASTING

The United Church of Christ has, under Parker's leadership, produced other kinds of programs as well. "All Aboard for Adventure" was a series of fifty-two children's programs designed to teach about human life, needs, and mission endeavors in foreign lands. The series gained exposure during prime children's time because the networks were looking for children's programs at the time.

Parker and his staff no longer do any programming for television or radio in protest against broadcast industry practices. His fight with the industry is discussed in fuller detail below (Chapter 7). Basically, he contends that current policies limit religious programming in prime time to spots of less than a minute, which, he argues, is a "denial of access" to the airways. One cannot teach humans or enhance their life-style or character in a few seconds of clever gimmickry.

Parker is vigorously committed to forcing the broadcast industry to be responsible to human spiritual and moral needs. To be responsible, he believes, they must provide substantial prime time weekly for extended and in-depth treatment of the claims of Christ on personal and social character, quality, patterns, and styles.

The Southern Baptist Convention

Paul M. Stevens, who runs the Radio and Television Commission (RTC) for the Southern Baptist Convention—without a doubt the finest religious broadcasting operation in existence—would demur at being called a religious broadcaster. He sees himself rather as a "broadcaster who produces mainly religious material." Whatever one calls him, his ministry, headquartered in Fort Worth, reaches around the world with an amazingly varied barrage of radio and television programs. The objective of each is to teach the doctrine and ethics of Christianity in a way that makes it both attractive and believable. There is an urgency about this for him.

> One hundred million television sets are turned on in America every evening.... Television and radio are so undisturbed by Christianity that one must ultimately believe that man does live by bread along—and toothpaste—and cars—and aspirin—and gad-

gets, gadgets, gadgets! The enemies of Christ are not silent. They are employing the mass media to reach people with ideologies that are non-Christian and spiritually destructive.[4]

Since their withdrawal from the SRRC in 1949, the Southern Baptists have had a history of independent denominational broadcasting rather than ecumenical endeavors. But the religious programs prepared by the RTC have a broad scope of appeal and relevance, and are tailored to a variety of specific audiences, interest groups, and needs. Broadcasts are aired in ten different languages—including Russian, Portuguese, Italian, Chinese, and Spanish—and are sent into the homelands of these groups. Technically, the programs are near perfect. Stevens himself has the style, ability, and charisma that would allow him to compete with the great broadcast preachers of any decade or the famous evangelists of the Sinai spectacles. But he has chosen instead to teach, to employ the broadcasting media as his podium and stage for instruction. To examine the results is to be convinced he has made the right choice.

It took time for the RTC to develop the success it has achieved today. When Stevens began, broadcasters were amused. As he tells it,

> Southern Baptists have been one of the most berated, mistreated, and maligned denominations in America. ... The first time I went into the office of a vice-president of a broadcasting company and told him who I was, he very kindly and gently said, "Now Southern Baptists, are they the foot-washing Baptists?" I said, "No! Not at all." I took *books* and gave them to key people in the networks which informed them of our denomination. We presented *programs* which informed them about our denomination's thrust and sense of responsibility. We put our Executive Secretary before them, some of our best ministers were exposed to them, our denominational executives were placed on panels and used to inform the networks about us.[5]

The public relations efforts worked and the denomination's image and influence were enhanced. The RTC began its national television ministry in 1954 by producing a series of films intended to give modern-day life to the

---

[4]Promotional brochure, "The Radio and Television Commission of the Southern Baptist Convention," Jan. 1968.
[5]Personal interview with the author.

parables of Christ. The first was "This My Son" about the prodigal son. Twenty-nine more filmed parables were to follow in the next three years, and these were released for television distribution as the series "This Is the Answer." A series of repeat showings was released in 1960, but that marked the termination of the parable format. The series "This Is the Answer" was continued through 1970, using drama and documentary formats, and eventually producing nearly 150 television films, which subsequently have become available for cable (CATV) television.

An arrangement had been concluded early in the production and distribution of the Parables series, which gave the Southern Baptist Convention possession and use of the films after their network airing. In 1958 a program called "televangelism" was initiated through private distribution of the Parables films. Church organizations in each market area were organized as viewing and discussion centers (similar to Parker's use of "Tangled World" in 1968-69). Unchurched and non-Christian people from every community were invited to these households or church parlors to view and discuss the films being televised according to a preannounced schedule. The objective was to foster growth in Christian insight, understanding, and faith commitment. The program, which ran for five years, is considered by Stevens to have been one of the most successful projects ever undertaken by RTC.[6]

As taste in programming shifted in the early 1960s, RTC changed its format from the parables to documentary and drama. It has remained with these since, adding children's cartoon dramas and some spot broadcasting.

During the 1960s, RTC produced, in conjunction with the three networks, a dozen one-hour specials, four of which were eventually rerun, and a long list of half-hour

---

[6]*Ibid.* The United Methodist Church produced and aired a series called "Breakthrough" during the 1960's. It was designed almost exactly like the televangelism program, except that instead of employing half-hour films, it distributed fifteen-minute films of a panel-documentary type format intended to lead into a discussion by the viewers. It was also distributed for in-church use. It was not considered effective, though the standards by which the Methodists judged audience effect were probably erroneous. The program seemed more effective on the local level than the producers judged.

films, many of them aired on the National Council of Churches series, "Directions," "Lamp Unto My Feet," and "Frontiers of Faith." The majority of these specials were produced in color.

Some of the one-hour specials were worship services from large Baptist churches. Others were dramas. "The Inheritance" (the story of the Old Testament) and "The Vine" (the life of Christ) are considered among the finest one-hour specials of any kind ever presented on network television. Along with "Walk Beside Me," which follows the footsteps of Paul through the Mediterranean world, these form a highly competent trilogy of filmed Christian instruction. *"Ecce Homo,"* a treatment of human history through scenes from the British Museum in London, and aired by NBC on January 5, 1969, and February 1, 1970, also received excellent critical notice.

The thirty-minute specials produced by Stevens in cooperation with the networks make up a very long list. A few of them have been dramas. Among the more significant of these have been "Battleground," concerning a college boy's search for his own identity; "The Legacy," about the struggle of a minister to relate to his own family; and "The Alchemy of Love," which deals with the influence of Christianity in the life of Robert Browning and the buoyant, optimistic faith that pervades his poetry. The documentary series of thirty-minute films includes "Zarethan" and "Of Picks, Shovels, and Words" (both on biblical archaeology), "The Seven Cities" and "I, John," dealing with the last book of the Bible, and the biographical "Aunt Clara" and "The Roads to Heaven." In addition a number of films in a variety of different modes were produced. A group of films designed as interviews, dialogues, semi-biographies, arts presentations, and musicals were produced and aired in cooperation with the networks.

Paul Stevens has appeared in interviews with numerous leading personalities in government, industry, and the church. The most notable of these was, perhaps, an intensive and revealing conversation with Malcolm Muggeridge taped in November 1969 in London. It later developed into an ABC special. On June 14, 1970, Stevens and Muggeridge were featured in another special on ABC.

MODELS OF RELIGIOUS BROADCASTING

The RTC's primary efforts in television broadcasting have been series, most prominent of which are "The Answer," "The Human Dimension," and "Jot." In 1973 "The Answer" was playing on 92 English and Spanish stations each week. No new episodes were being introduced, but the numerous existing films were still enjoying "wide acceptance."[7]

On January 1, 1972, the syndicated series "The Human Dimension" was introduced. The plan for this series of documentary and dramatic films dealing with contemporary problems is to film thirteen episodes each year, to be aired on public service time.

The first titles in the series suggest Stevens' insistent ambition to teach. "Treaties" is a documentary about an American Indian, once a "peyote priest" and alcoholic, who explains his efforts to bridge the gap between his people's heritage and their future in America through Christianity. "Operation Nightwatch" describes the pooling of efforts by ministers from a number of faith groups and theological traditions to help the down and out on Seattle's Skid Row. The practical, ethical questions of new surgical techniques are featured in "Organ Transplant," in which Drs. Michael DeBakey and Denton Cooley appear in real-life hospital scenes.

"Jot" is a five-minute full-color cartoon insert that can be dropped into children's commercial cartoon programs. It is Stevens' moral, spiritual, and educational counterattack on the Saturday morning violence of television. It is not intended for broadcast as a titled program with a denominational tag line, but as just another cartoon segment. "Jot" first appeared nationally on ten stations in 1968. It has expanded to regular scheduling on over a hundred major market stations, and has already produced high mail response from viewers.[8]

"Jot" is an effort at diversification, at reaching a dis-

---

[7] Jo Darden, letter to author dated March 8, 1973.

[8] The Lutheran series called "Davey and Goliath" is a cartoon drama with pedagogical objectives designed very much like "Jot" though it is a fifteen-minute format. The LCA series is very popular and might also be selected as illustration of the "podium" employment of religious broadcasting.

tinct audience—children under ten years—who could only be reached in regular programming at the cost of diluting the product. "Jot" (which "stars" an animated dot) features a follow-up paper with scriptural teaching content. It is free to all stations for use on public service time.[9] By spring 1973 "Jot" had eighteen episodes and had gone international. Its Spanish equivalent, *"Puntito,"* appeared on twelve Spanish stations, as well as being used by the Baptist foreign missionaries in Mexico and Central America.

The RTC distributes its television programs in a variety of ways. "The Answer" series and the specials have been distributed through network arrangements and through the Broadcasting and Film Commission of the National Council of Churches. Some of these were subsequently syndicated privately, particularly in the "televangelism" program. "The Human Dimension" and "Jot" have been privately distributed, station by station. But nearly all RTC broadcasting has been public service programming. Stevens notes that the Southern Baptist Convention has never aired national religious television on purchased time, nor have RTC programs ever solicited a dime on the air.

By his programs of confrontation, lecture, documentary, discussion, interview, cartoon, drama, and illustration, Stevens has probably achieved more than any other American religious broadcaster. Yet his annual budget is only 25% more than that, for example, of "The Back to God Hour," which is limited to a preaching ministry on radio. RTC has nearly 2500 broadcasts a week. Stevens' preference for the teaching model has prompted him to use mostly half-hour and hour programs. He insists that "program length should be determined by the subject not the time frame of the station program." Until 1970, RTC was the only producer of religious programming to do hour programs, which they began in 1963.

To teach theology is the main objective. The length of the program is conditioned by the particular theological message and what it requires. The mode that best expresses that message, in the judgment of RTC specialists, is the

---

[9]SBC-RTC "Programming Marketing Bulletin," for "Jot."

mode selected. Since it takes time and sustained impact to instruct a man in the Christian way, the longer programs predominate. Since the parable, drama, and documentary effectively teach the Christian way, those styles predominate.

Stevens gears the theology he teaches to the expectations of the denomination that is supporting him:

> Our denomination is an evangelistic and fundamental denomination. We seek to be anything but liberal in our approach to the Word of God or to man's state in this world, and man's relationship with God today. I felt that we needed to treat man within. We do not intend to imply that we can ignore man's life context but that it is crucial to begin with the question of the *quality* of that life. We wish to help make a *new* man. . . . We concentrate on man's renewal in Jesus Christ.

Given the relative affluence of the RTC and the continuing growth of the Southern Baptist Convention—in the face of decline in other churches—economics have never been a serious problem for Stevens. Still, the RTC tries not "to duplicate programs where others are spending the Lord's money successfully." Success in spending money is not measured by how much is bought per dollar, but how much audience impact is realized per dollar. Getting to the desired audience in its prime viewing time with a message that produces the desired consequence is the objective. Weighing that against cost shapes the economic issue. Stevens states:

> I was convinced from the beginning that you get more audience per dollar with drama than any other type of format available. When we went into drama that was the era of the great dramas. . . . When your audience is tuned to a certain type of format, programming is like catching a freight train. You run straight at it and get destroyed, run against its direction and never grab hold, or run with it and step aboard. Following trends is as crucial to religious broadcasters as to anyone else. A trend represents a public frame of mind. If you are going to take advantage of the times in which you live you are doing nothing more than the Apostle John using apocalyptic literature for the "Revelation of St. John." That was the style of the day. We try to discover what it is to which the public is listening and design our programs within the framework of that mind-set or life-style.

Stevens feels that trying to buy television time would weaken rather than strengthen the RTC's thrust. Most television stations—especially network affiliates—are reluctant to sell the time anyway. There are simply too many denominations and faith groups clamoring for the exposure, and the stations prefer to leave the decisions to the network. In the face of that situation the RTC has adopted the philosophy that they can accomplish more if they do not worry about whether they get credit for it:

> Any time [the industry] wants any religious material, signed or unsigned, sponsored or unsponsored, we will produce it. We do traffic safety spots, brotherhood spots, United Fund spots with a spiritual point of view, United Nations Day spots, crippled children spots. We give them to them free.... We produce floods of material of this type.... We have provided the Public Safety Department of the State of North Carolina traffic safety spots for the major holidays of the year..., the only return to us being the fact that we are part of the North Carolina broadcasting industry.

Small wonder that Stevens gets nearly $10 million worth of free public service time annually from grateful broadcasters.

Seventh-Day Adventist Church

One of the great success stories in religious broadcast history is "Faith for Today," since 1950 the international television ministry of the Seventh-Day Adventists. Its star is the skilled and durable William A. Fagal.

"Faith for Today" was the first network television program sponsored by any denomination. It was conceived and is funded by a denomination that was in 1950 not generally considered to represent mainstream Protestantism nor American ecclesiastical power. Its religious broadcaster has been the same man (with his family) throughout the program's long history. Its format has been an imaginative and innovative teaching style from the beginning. The program has a number of "firsts" to its credit: it was the first religious feature program in Australia, Guam, and Nigeria; the first non-government-sponsored Protestant, religious telecast in South America. In 1956 it was one of the first religious programs to switch from live broadcast to film packaging; in 1963 it became the first religious telecast to move to color production.[10]

Fagal was born in Albany on January 17, 1919. He graduated in theology from Atlantic Union College at age 20 and entered the Seventh-Day Adventist ministry. Following early pastorates in Elmira and Buffalo, New York, he moved to Brooklyn in 1944, accepting a pastorate that included a broadcast ministry called "The Bible Auditorium of the Air." Under Fagal's direction it became a weekly ministry to the East Coast.

Fagal's considerable experience in broadcasting and his natural talent for pastoring led his denomination to tap his highly developed skills in 1950, when television became a functional tool. The denomination furnished total and enthusiastic support for the ministry from the beginning.

There is no end in sight for Fagal's broadcast ministry or for his effectiveness in it. "Faith for Today" is currently broadcast over nearly two hundred television stations in the United States alone. Its international ministry is equally impressive. In a continually new and creative way Fagal teaches his convictions concerning the nature of his Christian way. Without flamboyance and emotional sensationalism, his sensible, humane confrontation of humanity works to change the quality and character of human lives.

Fagal is usually joined in his television broadcast by his attractive wife. Together they develop the program style and message in a family-like discussion experience. The setting is low-key, informal, human.

> Hands folded simply atop a well-worn Morocco leather Bible, William A. Fagal looks directly into the lens of the softly whirring motion picture camera; and in a voice that bespeaks confidence, conviction, and compassion, seeks to bring spiritual aid and comfort to the millions who address him simply as "Pastor."[11]

First on the program is a five-minute sermonette. Then follows any of a wide variety of events for the next

---

[10]Roger W. Coon, "The Public Speaking of Dr. William A. Fagal of 'Faith for Today,' America's First National Television Pastor."
[11]Ibid., p. 130.

twenty-two minutes. Illustrations of a life setting or a graphically portrayed idea, an interview with a noted person, a discussion with his wife—whatever the choice, the result is instructive and interesting. Whether or not one identifies readily with the content, the style is attractive.

Surely a major reason for the continuing appeal of "Faith for Today" to the millions who watch it is the personal qualities of Fagal, transmitted well by the television camera. He comes across as a warm and approachable man. He evidences an honest interest in the persons with whom he visits by means of television. People trust him for this. Moreover, he has mental acuity. He is not an "egghead," but he makes no apology for being intellectually sharp and able to range widely and intelligently in his discussions.

Fagal's technical skill as television performer is important to his success in communicating a natural style and believable message. He has a vibrant sense of humor and laughs easily. Whether he is performing a brief dramatic skit, conducting an interview with the Archbishop of Canterbury, or talking with his wife, he has "presence," colorful flair, and authentic naturalness. Fagal projects integrity. He is neither maudlin nor haughty. He is transparently honest in his conviction that

> That which has been accomplished through "Faith for Today" has been the result of nothing but Heaven's blessings. . . . God has used the poorest of instruments, making the maximum in mistakes, to accomplish something for His name's honor and glory.[12]

Neither Fagal nor the Seventh-Day Adventist Church had a clear idea at the outset regarding the best format or program style.[13] However, both were convinced that the program objective had to be the *teaching* of the Christian faith. Network officials had indicated that the stereotyped radio format of "preach-sing-pray" would be poor television programming.

[12] William A. Fagal, "May 21, 1950: A Memorable Day," *Telenotes*, May 1965, p. 5.
[13] Gordon F. Dalrymple, "Fifteen Years of Progress," *Telenotes*, May 1965, p. 3; see also Coon, *op. cit.*, p. 162.

They were... "very much opposed to the conventional church-service-type program, and complained, 'Here's one of the greatest means of communication in the world, and no one with anything to say!' "[14]

The network people suggested that a dramatic format be used. It was to become the style of the 1950s, but no one had used it significantly in religious television. Fagal was ready to try it. He thought there were things about the Christian gospel which might relate well to dramatic television. Christ had used parables impressively, and Fagal supposed that television drama might be turned into twentieth-century Christian parables.

> Realizing that TV audiences appreciate more action than a pulpit alone could possibly afford, we discarded the preaching type program that we had used in radio. Our TV program was planned around a dramatic problem-discussion sketch, a male quartet to sing favorite hymns, closing with a short, direct, into-the-camera sermon that would summarize the points which had been discussed.
>
> Our first budget was so meager that we had no writers, no professional actors; as a matter of fact, we had nothing but a dream and the realization that a way must be found to use television effectively for the spread of the gospel.[15]

The program was soon billed as "The Family Religious Telecast," because the first program opened with the Fagal family in a home-like setting. The children were then "hustled off to bed," since it was 9:30 p.m.; and William and Virginia Fagal began a discussion. That opening gambit with the children paid unexpectedly handsome—and permanent—dividends. Viewers began to write to the Fagals, telling them about *their* families. Having seen the Fagal family on the screen, viewers felt they knew them as personal friends.

The family segment was relatively short and pointed. The camera then switched to a pastor's study stage set. Fagal was there. A young doctoral student from Columbia walked in, discouraged about his future and the meaning-

---

[14]Coon, *op. cit.*, p. 162.
[15]"Yes, Indeed, TV Is Well Worthwhile, " *Telenotes*, May 1955, p. 2.

lessness of his life. Fagal began an informal conversation with the young man, and gradually developed an exposition of the second coming of Christ. It was designed, clearly, to teach a Christian view of the purpose, future, and hope of life. With him Fagal had a replica of the image described in Daniel 2, and he resorted to his visual aid often for illustration in the conversation with the student.

Fagal told Roger Coon that "Faith for Today" has always been shaped by four specific objectives: (1) to do away with the negative image of Seventh-Day Adventists in the public mind; (2) to destroy "Mother Hubbard" stereotypes of the Christian missionary overseas; (3) to gain new members for the denomination; (4) to interest viewers in the Bible.[16] There is no mention of the Seventh-Day Adventist Church during the program itself—only in a credit line at the end. Between 1950 and 1973, however, Fagal's ministry added more than twenty-five thousand members to his denomination.

This is not to say that no shadows have ever fallen across the stage of "Faith for Today." Between 1957 and 1959 there was a sudden decline in the number of stations and desirable time slots carrying the program. From 162 stations Fagal dropped to 125. There were five reasons. First, a number of other professionally produced religious programs finally arose to compete with Fagal, most significantly, the Missouri Synod Lutherans' "This Is the Life." Second, Fagal had no field sales-promotion representatives. Third, stations were able to sell as much of their time as they wished to commercial interests, so they relegated the least desirable time to religious programs, which might not increase audience size. Fourth, new broadcast industry policies moved away from the idea of selling air time to religious institutions, while at the same time allocating public service time mainly through local councils of churches, leaving independent broadcasters like Fagal in a difficult competitive position. Fifth, rates for time available for purchase increased as much as 80% between 1954 and 1964.

But throughout it all—crisis and success—Fagal has

---

[16]Coon, *op. cit.*, p. 173, quoting an interview with Fagal on July 5, 1966.

adapted, planned, and kept on programming. His first format could be called a drama-variety design. He soon turned often to interviews with dignitaries, missionaries, and government leaders, invariably asking them why they as Christians had chosen their particular vocation. A third type of program was the travelogue. Fagal himself shot much of the film on location all over the world. Whether in Bible lands, on a floating hospital on the Amazon, with foreign missionaries on the field, or at disaster sites—he caught "slices of life" where the action was. From travelogue he moved in 1959 to a musical program by the "Faith for Today" quartet. In 1966 he added the "illustrated sermon."

All of these program types were interchanged week by week, year in and year out. Something new was always happening, and yet it was always the same. It was always the remarkable William Fagal, teaching the Christian faith in everyday, down-to-earth terms.

No one has been more durable in religious television. Few have been more flexible in imagination and teaching skill. Many have copied Fagal's style, but none with the natural approachableness of the "pastor next door."

There is no end in sight for Fagal's broadcast ministry or his effectiveness in it. "Faith for Today" is currently broadcast over nearly two hundred stations in the United States alone. Its international ministry is equally impressive. In a continually new and creative way Fagal teaches his convictions concerning the nature of the Christian way. Without flamboyance or emotionalism, his sensible, humane confrontation of his viewers works to change the quality and character of human lives.

Lutheran Church—Missouri Synod

One of the best-known Protestant efforts in religious television has been "This Is the Life," sponsored by the Lutheran Church—Missouri Synod since 1951. "This Is the Life" is a religious situational drama that endeavors to "stage real-life joy, relief, and other human experiences," which can readily be seen as relating to the human religious quest. Each drama is specifically focused in a theological message. The program primarily features the Fisher family, and plays out the drama of the needs and hopes, fears and faith of the members.

The Lutherans' strong interest in television ministry dates back to 1948, before television had even become a functional opportunity for religious broadcasting. Anticipation of a great broadcasting future was vigorously alive in the imagination of many church members.

In 1949 the Synod was petitioned for funds for the development of television programs. Walter Maier of "The Lutheran Hour" radio ministry hailed television as a new medium for preaching, and for a brief time the production of pulpit-oriented television was contemplated. Under the leadership of Herman W. Gockel—and impressed by the copies of programs they had seen produced by William Fagal in the dramatic format—the Lutherans set aside the influence of their great broadcast preacher in favor of televised drama.

As a result of the early and sustained success of the half-hour series, the Lutherans have confined their national television ministry to that one program, except for a few specials produced in recent years. This decision has been reinforced by the overriding objective of the church to teach theology in its broadcast ministry. The constituency in the denomination has proved itself willing to pay for this relatively costly program style. Until 1968 the entire budget for "This Is the Life" came from the denomination. Since then, there has also been considerable support from the Lutheran Layman's League, enabling the program to avoid further curtailments in an age of upward-spiraling costs. The budget for the program is well over a million dollars a year. For many years "This Is the Life" offered twenty-six episodes each year; and, by the use of reruns, aired fifty-two annually. After 1964, budgetary considerations cut annual production to twenty-one programs a year. In 1971 and 1972 this was reduced further and some new formats tentatively researched.

During its fifteenth anniversary year (1967) the program switched to full-color production. By that time it was seen by about fifteen million people a week on 380 American and Canadian stations, as well as Armed Forces Television and in eight foreign countries. Three 13-week series with sound tracks in Spanish, French, and Portuguese were completed.

> By this time the Lutheran Television Productions had accumulated a library of some four hundred Christian message films. To insure maximum use of the films, it divided them into three different series for release to television outlets in multiple station areas. These films were retitled and soon appeared in TV guides throughout the country under the titles "The Fisher Family," "Patterns for Living," and "This Is the Life."[17]

By the end of 1967 over one hundred of these films had been released for in-church educational use by fifteen hundred congregations, as well as institutions like prisons, hospitals, and civic and service clubs.

In its first fifteen years the series received twelve Freedom Foundation awards, two General Federation of Women's Clubs awards, three National Safety Council awards, a Christian Youth Cinema award, a National Women's Research Guild award, and two *Billboard* magazine awards.

That kind of success, in the Lutherans' case, has not just happened. That the church has maintained its dramatic format in religious telecasting from the beginning is no mere coincidence. Gockel's rationale for the format is precisely stated, full of theological conviction as well as technical sophistication and carefully reasoned communications theory and practice. Some may disagree with his arguments, but it is difficult to explain away his results.

Unless the screen is used to portray action—rather than talking, preaching, lecturing—Gockel has always believed, it is not being properly used. From that decision at the outset, "we played it by ear," he says:

> The drama should be built on stories that have inherent problems in them which reflect a crucial spiritual matter. These problems have to be the kind with which the average human can identify directly and immediately. The problem needs a good and authentic crisis, struggle, and resolution.... We try to get problems relevant to people, offering solutions with which the listeners and viewers can empathetically identify.[18]

[17] Herman Gockel, "Historical Material on 'This Is the Life,' " pp. 5f. See also A. William Bluem, *Religious Television Programs*, p. 30.
[18] Personal interview with the author.

Gockel's chief support base among the Missouri Lutherans is a conservative, evangelical one. The aim of Lutheran Television Productions programming is thus to convey more than mere moralism or theism. A consequence of this, Gockel argues, is that somewhere in the program the gospel must be verbalized.

> That is the *skandalon*, the stumbling stone, in our approach. I know of no other way of imparting to the unconverted, unconcerned, unchurched viewer the message of the grace of God in Christ than by using words.... The camera will not pick up the essential message we want to deliver. It will need to be picked up by the microphone. Somebody is going to have too *say* something that is different, distinctive. Someone is going to have to mention Christ and his grace.

This does not mean, Gockel emphasizes, that the programs must or should resort to clichés, Bible texts, or doctrinal formulas.

The theological objective cannot be attained, however, unless the program has dramatic integrity. The character in the drama who verbalizes the gospel must do so convincingly in the context of the action. If the viewer is given the impression that the verbalization of the gospel by the character is merely tacked into the fabric of the action as a commercial by the sponsor, the program will be dead as far as achieving its evangelical purpose is concerned.

In line with his theological rationale, Gockel points out that not all good Christian stories are suitable for the program. He uses as an example an episode of "The Fisher Family" that was filmed, but which did not—and indeed *could* not—have what Gockel considers to be both the requisite authenticity and the needed evangelical message. Carl Fisher is urged to run for public office. Although he is disinclined to do so, his friends say it is his moral duty. So he goes to his pastor for advice. That is where the problem arises for evangelical television drama, Gockel claims. Talking to a well-indoctrinated layman in that context, the minister

> is merely going to speak about Carl's obligation as a Christian to be salt, to be a light, to get out there and spread the salt, let the light shine. That is good evangelical admonition, but it is not really a statement of the gospel. Theologically, we would classify that in Lutheran systematics as sanctification, not justification.

> We do our best job when we stick close to justification.... After the American gets into a church he can hear more about the Christian in politics. I want to get him to an awareness of his need for a Savior.

Gockel affirms without apology that his characters must struggle with life's vertical dimension. His characters must live life as in the presence of the righteous, redemptive God. They must be brought through the dramatic processes of guilt, grace, and gratitude. "That is good drama and good theology. We do not want cheap grace."[19] An effort is made to have every drama consciously Cross-centered—an effort that is successful about ninety percent of the time, he feels.

In addition to the theological justification for the dramatic format, Gockel continues to assume that the television screen is best suited to drama, though he does not attempt to justify the assumption that the format he has chosen is better for television than documentaries, interviews, discussions, or spots. No doubt it is true that in the early 1950s, when the program was coming into its own, drama was the most prominent and effective form of television broadcasting. Although that emphasis receded in the 1960s, "This Is the Life" did not change. Some observers of the medium would suggest that the pendulum is now swinging back to drama.

Not to be disregarded in considering format is the acceptance by station managers of the program as it is. According to Gockel, there are really only two reasons why more than four hundred station managers carry "This Is the Life" each week—quality and dependability. He says:

> By quality I mean that we are a professionally produced series.... We are a slick production.... By dependability I mean that they know that every Wednesday . . . they are going to have a reel of "This Is the Life." If they wish they can preview it. Most do not, since they know our quality and dependability.... We have never embarrassed any station.... We are to religious broadcasting what Prudential is to life insurance.

---

[19]*Ibid.*; cf. Gockel, "Some Basic Factors Governing the Church's Use of Mass Media," pp. 3f.

To discuss format is a waste of time unless one has station manager acceptance in the first place, Gockel argues. Most station managers when selecting public service programs aim for those which are mediocre at best. The advantage of "This Is the Life" to station managers is that the dramatic format holds the audience for the following commercially sponsored programs, whose rating really matters in an economic sense.

Finances, as mentioned above, do not influence program format, especially as the backlog of programs increases and allows for repeated reruns in any sequence. Thus, the producers can react to increases or decreases in the budget by increasing or cutting back the number of new productions per year rather than having to switch to a less expensive format.

Around the television broadcasts, Lutheran Television Productions has developed a comprehensive program to insure their continued impact. The program itself is designed to dramatize the power of the gospel in true-to-life situations. Along with this, an offer of printed materials is made to interested viewers. Third, a system has been developed which enables the St. Louis office to forward all incoming mail to selected centers around the country, which in turn distribute each letter to the local pastor nearest the inquirer. This efficient follow-through system has been operative since the program began.

Martin J. Neeb, Jr., the current head of the Missouri Synod television ministry, has a great appreciation for what his denomination has accomplished in the field of religious broadcasting. He is concerned about the future of religious television.

> The "This Is the Life" format has been one of the great mainstays in religious television.... We have been searching for an even better way for the last ten years. We recognize that somehow people always assume that a given format or technique "runs out of gas." ... We have been looking for another effective format, but in ten years of diligent research we have not found anything to replace the drama effectively.[20]

---

[20] Personal interview with the author, April 1972.

Neeb's judgment is bolstered by the consistent outreach of "This Is the Life" to five million middle-aged or older church members and non-church members per week across the nation. As a "shotgun" impact, that is hard to beat on a cost-per-thousand basis. "This Is the Life" costs $10.00 per thousand viewers and has received five million dollars worth of free time from 260 stations in the United States alone. Neeb says:

> This is just about the most efficient mission opportunity that the church has. I do not know of any church body that contacts people on behalf of the Christian gospel at so low a cost. It is a highly efficient way of reaching people.[21]

While many mainline Protestant and Catholic organizations have moved toward spot broadcasting as the format for the 1970s, Neeb has followed Paul Stevens' example and moved toward hour-long network specials as the wave of the future. It is a way to get the gospel into prime time—where the general audience is. The Lutherans' first effort was in the area of children's programming.

> We looked at the Peanuts specials and noticed that over a period of five years, not only were they immensely successful with families, but they also gained in their audience potential from year to year. The reruns were even more popular than the original airings. The Peanuts Specials were animation, which is costly. But if you can run a program repeatedly for five years, it is economical. Moreover, we noticed the holiday children's programs draw the heaviest total audience of anything in the history of television.[22]

Lutheran Television Productions created a series of "Christmas Is" type specials, featuring Benji, a ten-year-old schoolboy who is used as a vehicle to tell the nativity story. Benji is accompanied by his dog Waldo as they are transported, in the mind's eye, back to the first Christmas.

> Benji and Waldo experience excitement and some tense moments as they encounter Roman centurions, the innkeeper and crowds of travelers, Mary and Joseph, the shepherds and, finally, the Christ child in the manger. When Benji has met the real second shepherd, and been impressed by the significance of the events he

---

[21] Personal interview with the author, July 1973.
[22] *Ibid.*

ELECTRONIC EDUCATION

has witnessed, he has a new understanding of the season. He wakes from his reverie, proud and eager to perform his role. And the school play takes place, enlivened by the byplay and high jinks of today's boys and girls.[23]

The special—a top-quality Hollywood production—was released on film as an ideal family program for Advent. It featured Hans Conried with a professional staff of production people, a completely original musical score, and two new Christmas songs.

A special feature of the marketing procedure was the arrangement for the station to sell commercial time during the hour special, which made it doubly desirable to station managers. With such an excellent package to offer to the stations, Neeb insisted on and got prime time or near-prime time. It was seen on 479 broadcasts in 1972, and produced over 175,000 requests for the record given away as a "follow-up" ministry. Comic books were also mailed on request.

But there has been no resting on laurels at LTP. Easter 1973 featured "Easter Is," the second in this hour-long series of specials for prime time. The newest thing in Missouri Synod television is a move toward social-problem oriented programs. Programs on venereal disease and on drug abuse were released in 1972.

Neeb is as committed as his predecessor to Cross-centered programming. He insists on emphasizing "reconciliation through Christ."

> It doesn't do much good to talk about the situation if you're not going to be specifically gospel-oriented because that is what I believe actually holds the power to convert people. So we build the cross into every piece of our product. In addition, however, television is a great appetite builder and creates tremendous amounts of goodwill for the Lutheran Churches. "Christmas Is" brought many people to the Lutheran congregations because people said, "If that is what Lutherans are doing, I ought to take another look at the local Lutheran church."

Neeb works hard at integrating the broadcast with local church follow-up and mission endeavor.

The Lutheran Church—Missouri Synod knows very spe-

---

[23] Lutheran Television Productions, "Christmas Is" marketing flier.

cifically what message it wishes to teach. It has thoroughly researched teaching techniques for television, and decided that drama works best. It is willing to pay the price for that opportunity to teach the Christian way of faith and life. It has turned the microphone and camera into a podium for dramatic Christian education. The church thus stands solidly in the tradition of the parable pedagogy of the Rabbi from Nazareth.

six
A Little Leaven

The religious "spot" is a short message—nearly always less than a minute in length—which is not unlike a commercial advertisement in its format. Use of spots for religious television began in 1958 with the work of Caroline Rakestraw, a remarkable woman from Atlanta who has been responsible for many innovations in gospel communication during her tenure with the Division of Radio and Television of the Protestant Episcopal Church.

The first Episcopalian television ministry in the United States was a series of "Holy Day and Holiday" spots produced by Mrs. Rakestraw. They were one-minute color spots, built around series of slide photographs of the great art of Europe. The sound track related the scenes to the theme and theology of the holy days and holidays of the church. Spots were included for Easter, Christmas, Thanksgiving Day, Independence Day, and Labor Day, and these were later packaged on film. Both the slide series and the film packages were privately syndicated and used for church presentations. NBC picked up a number of the spots and gave them network distribution, though that was not the primary intent. The spots were run consistently during prime time.

In the early 1960s Dana Kennedy was employed by the Episcopal Church to produce a series of television spots called "Thought for the Day." These used a straightforward preach-teach format, with a clergyman talking directly into the camera to the viewer. The technique was not a creative one, and the results did not prove to be very popular, with the result that the series was not continued. But the church kept at it, and in 1970 a series of experiments in spots was kicked off by a remarkable production called "Spectator Sport." The script itself suggests the punch and impact the spot had. It appeared in twenty-, thirty-, and sixty-second formats:

> "There's a lot of trouble in this world."
> *(shot of a city burning and war erupting)*
>
> "There really is!"
> *(contemplative shot of a viewer)*
>
> "And you can't make it go away by switching channels."
> *(shot of blurred television screen)*
>
> "Being a Christian . . .
> *(shot of lions and Christians in Roman amphitheater)*
>
> " . . . didn't used to be a spectator sport."
> *(closeup of Roman Christians)*
>
> "It still isn't!"
> *(closeup of television viewer followed by tag identifying the broadcaster)*[1]

One station ran the spot in the middle of a nationally televised ball game.[2] Rev. Robert Libby, director of television programming for the Episcopal Church, was quoted by *TV Guide* as saying: "They're not very profound mes-

---

[1] DRTV promotional sheet, "New Public Service Television Spot."
[2] Richard K. Doan, "That Old Time Religion Brought Up To Date," *TV Guide*, Dec. 20, 1969.

sages but they get in and out quick, and make a point before anybody can tune out."³

The religious broadcasters who use spot television see it as a provocative form of teaching or producing insights in people. The churches that moved to this format, especially in the late 1960s, described it as a kind of social "leaven." The spot presents a short provocative idea that initiates constructive thought, feeling, and action in the viewer. It is seen as a twentieth-century form of the "Socratic dialogue," as a tool to introduce people into the new life that can be found only in Jesus Christ.

The use of spot television depends on acceptance of a specific theological assumption. A spot is designed to startle a viewer or listener with an idea, question, or issue. That will force him to think seriously and thus experience some growth in Christian concern, understanding, or action. The spot technique, therefore, assumes that the business of inciting humans to responsible godliness can be accomplished by confronting man with God's claim. That, in turn, assumes God to be immanent in his world—the world of man—and capable of confronting man, at least vicariously.

Moreover, the theology of the broadcast spot, very much like that of the pedagogical television programming considered in the previous chapter, assumes that man has the ability to grow through encounter with God's claim. Whether it hits him through the radio in his car or the color television in his den, the spot is intended to provoke unusually intense thought or feeling about a specific concern of Christian behavior. The matter so lodged in his feelings or thoughts is then expected to ferment like yeast and spring to life as a full-blown attitude, conviction, or action.

This theology takes God and man seriously. Its view of God is a high one: it sees him as the rightful governor of man's existence and the immanent divine presence, incarnated, as it were, in the human voice of the spot, redemptively addressing himself to man, who is, by implication, an

³*Ibid.* See also *Time*, Jan. 12, 1970.

agent capable of acting out God's claim and disciplining his decisions and actions in terms of godliness. There is potential cooperation between God and man as co-workers in the kingdom. That implied partnership is in keeping with what may be known of God in Jesus Christ. The content of some spots suggests that God occasionally needs to cajole man into dealing with the real questions of responsible godliness, but God is nonetheless represented as supportive of man in his quest for truth, meaning, and obedience, not a dangerous and threatening alien from another world.

The United Presbyterian Church

The United Presbyterian Church moved totally into the spot format in 1965 and remained there until very recently. A long list of twenty-, thirty-, and sixty-second spots were produced. Although their effectiveness has been difficult to assess, they did succeed in gaining prime time, often from the networks, and thus in reaching audiences not generally tuned to religious programs.

High on the list of reasons for the Presbyterians' use of spots was the economic question. Richard Gilbert and Charles Brackbill felt that spots provided the maximum audience at the lowest cost per viewer. In 1965 all mainline denominations were trying to expand their outreach while holding firmly on to their fiscal belts. To acquire maximum exposure of the church's message within the confines of limited budgets was crucial. Moreover, Gilbert had just arrived on the scene that year, and he was determined to succeed as the new director of broadcasting for the denomination.

As the 1960s turned into the 1970s, affluence turned into austerity in church funding. When the fiscal belts were tightened, ministries like television broadcasting were the first to feel the pinch. Meanwhile, commercial broadcasters had found it lucrative to shorten the length of commercial messages and pack more advertisements into each station break, thus giving over more and more of each hour to profit-making rather than program content. Consequently, many denominations found that the only economically feasible way out of deep ghetto time on radio and television was to grab the twenty-second public service spots that the stations occasionally offered in prime or near-prime time. Unlike Paul Stevens of the Southern Baptists and Martin Neeb of the Missouri Lutherans, broadcasting directors for the Presbyterians, Episcopalians, and Methodists were unable to get nearly unlimited funding for network specials.

The assignment of public service time is strictly at the discretion of the broadcasting industry. If a religious program provided to a station airs at 5:30 a.m. on Sunday, it is likely that the format and content have been considered by the station management as not comparable with commercial programming. This may reflect their assessment of the potential audience interest in the program's content or of the style of the program or of the technical skill with which it was put together. In any case the program is not going to command a very wide audience at that hour of the day.

Moreover, many denominations have become dissatisfied with programming that reaches only the people who are already committed Christians or churchgoers. They want to contact, capture, "sneak up on" the people who do not even consider Christianity as a live option. To get maximum exposure to such an audience means trying to get on the air when they are watching—for instance at 2:30 on Sunday afternoon, when the football game is on. To slip in a religious spot during time-outs for station breaks would reach a maximum audience desired. Some denominations decided that thirty seconds of prime time was better than an hour of ghetto time.

During the 1950s the United Presbyterians tried to achieve maximum audience impact by urging the Broadcasting and Film Council of the NCC to employ formats which would receive prime-time airing. But as money became less plentiful in the mid-1960s the drama, interview, and documentary format became less and less financially feasible. The problems of audience size and quality per dollar contributed heavily to motivating the Presbyterians to decrease their cooperation with the BFC and move toward independence and spot format.[4] They began to think more in terms of the audience they wanted to reach from a sociological and psychological point of view.

Before attracting the audience, of course, one must have attracted the attention of the broadcasting industry. This requires carefully marketing what one has produced to local station program managers. If that process is carried out with sophistication, the station will no doubt take a thirty-second spot and give it a variety of exposures at different times, some of them during prime time. This "maximum audience exposure" factor is intricately related to the economic reasoning behind the use of religious spots in preference to longer formats.

Per-minute production costs for spots are extremely high. Even the radio spots which the noted humorist and ad-man Stan Freberg did for the United Presbyterian Church in the 1960s cost thousands of dollars each—despite the fact that Freberg donated his creative efforts. Television spots today cost between ten and thirty thousand dollars to produce. Still, Brackbill argues, spots are not as expensive as programs of greater length. "The economic issue is simple and plain," he says. Sunday morning programs find

> no significant return in terms of audience impact. There are those who say that no time is bad time, that "the program finds its audience." ... An advertiser would not buy Sunday time, however, unless he could hook onto the football game. Why should the church use [Sunday morning] time? It is probably irresponsible stewardship.[5]

Broadcasters have learned that children are attracted by short takes, a lesson that is put to considerable educational effect in the well-known "Sesame Street." Producers claim that people have such brief attention spans that the communicator in today's world must hit and run. So, too, the religious spot tries to hit the prime-time, unchurched, unconcerned viewer (as Brackbill says) "so fast that the guy cannot make it to the refrigerator."

---

[4] Personal conversation between the author and Larry McMaster, cited in Ellens, "Program Format in Religious Television," p. 182.
[5] Personal interview with the author.

A LITTLE LEAVEN

Research has shown that spots do get the attention of people and can stimulate thinking about man's relationship to God and to his fellow man. Some spots, Russell Jolly admits, just will not "win any converts" or "change any minds"—spots on drug abuse or racism, for example. The hope behind these is that they "will tickle the conscience so that down the line in some crisis in an individual's life something will be recalled that lights something up."[6] Just as the commercial advertisement for margarine seeks to plant in the viewer's mind a seed that will activate him the next time he is at the refrigeration counter in the supermarket, so the "Good Samaritan" spot, for instance, seeks to instill in him the potential to act the part of the Good Samaritan the next time such a situation arises. Alternatively, Thomson claims,

> The spot may reinforce something he did that day that was Christian. It may reinforce or clarify the fact that this principle was articulated by Christ, and that being *for* Christ's way means being a Good Samaritan. It may also clarify for him that Christ's sacrifice of himself was this kind of process.[7]

Hard sell is not appropriate technique for conveying such truths. The mandate for religious broadcasters, Thomson claims, is soft sell, the soft sell of leaven that will change attitudes, minds, feelings, actions, characters.

Given its length, the spot cannot indulge itself in the luxury of syllogisms or debate. "The name of the game," Brackbill says, "is emotion. We must touch the feeling world of people." The constant effort is to appeal to the whole person in redemptive Christian fashion.

> The problem is not to think up ideas and catchy situations but to understand what we really must do with them to make them effective. What behavioral objectives guide us? What action do we expect out of all this? What new thought do we want accepted in the process?

Modern man has lost his faith in Jesus Christ. Thoroughly secular, he is unmoved by appeals to his fear of the unknown or of death or of ultimate destiny. The church is irrelevant; its message a cliché that means nothing. It is the

---

[6]Personal interview with the author.
[7]Personal interview by the author with Mr. Robert Thomson, UPUSA.

MODELS OF RELIGIOUS BROADCASTING

duty of the religious broadcaster, Brackbill maintains, to reach that kind of audience with the message of Jesus Christ.

> The first thing for us is to find a point of reference.... To communicate with anyone you must touch something that already exists in him.... The second thing we must do is suggest some possibilities. That puts us in the clue, hint, parable business.... Television spots are essentially parables.... The third thing we must do is demonstrate.... The fourth thing we must do is to suggest some reasonable doubt about the prevailing value system with regard to human satisfaction and peace.

The church's business in the mass media, Brackbill believes, is not to impose on people a set of prefabricated answers to questions they have not asked, but to inject into the total pattern of their cultural, social, and intellectual experience some information that will have redemptive, leavening effect on their life and thought. What is communicated is an experience, *in whatever means or medium that succeeds.* Communication is two-way: the viewer or listener must respond to what the communicator says. This concept of proclamation is rooted in God's stooping to conquer, in his incarnating himself, not so much as Lord but as servant.

This does not mean that the church abandons authority. The church should speak out on moral issues, Brackbill believes, because it is the only institution that can speak with any authority. The touchy question is the manner in which it does this.

> Where else shall we go for our standards except to "Thus saith the Lord"—but in the posture and perspective of *grace?* There is no question that the job of the church is to speak the truth, unapologetically, but in love. We can bring people one step further along in their growth into what they ought to be. That spells success for us.

The Franciscans

Some of the most impressive work in religious spot broadcasting is being done by the Franciscan Order. Their communications center in Los Angeles, under the direction of Father Emery Tang, employs a staff of 55 to produce radio and television spots and educational films. Most of the staff are from the laity, and not all are Catholics. There are also six priests, six nuns, a couple of ex-nuns, and a Presbyterian minister whose job is marketing.

Tang himself is a colorful figure, a bald priest of Chinese extraction who looks like Yul Brynner and often signs the latter's autograph. He dresses in nonconformist style and has been called "the world's most turned-on monk." He has been featured on the talk-show circuit with Mike Douglas, Steve Allen, and Virginia Graham. As for television, his objectives are weighty but clear:

> What turns him on is film, and its potential as a tool to deliver the Judeo-Christian message. He is as moved by 60 seconds of inspired film as some clerics would be by a passage from the Bible. "Each age brings new developments, new insights," he explains. "You can't stand still. We're preaching the word just like Christ said to do. And this is the best way available. It's the means today. If the church could sponsor the finest in human endeavor—science and philosophy—through a world TV satellite system, then she'd be doing her job: to teach people."[8]

Like Gilbert and Brackbill, the Franciscans are committed to capturing choice seconds of prime time to suggest to post-Christian America that Christianity remains as a live option for rational people. Father Tang thinks of the religious spot as not so much a modern parable as a mini-morality play.

The Franciscans are concerned to communicate hope and inspiration through their "Telespots." They assume that people feel despair and loss of meaning today more than any other emotion. "Telespots" startle harried viewers to attention and then implant a seed of thought that may later blossom with purpose, meaning, and peace for those who get the message.

More than 750 stations in the United States, nearly 300 in Canada, and about 50 in Australia have carried the Franciscans' spots. The spots do not push Roman Catholicism or employ pressure techniques to get "conversions." Rather, they call humans to think, to reflect. They assume

---

[8]Joseph Finnigan, "The Spiritual Soft Sell of Father Emery Tang," *TV Guide*, Mar. 18, 1972, pp. 45f.

that most humans are sensible and capable of receiving healing insight if given the appropriate spiritual stimulation.

The soft sell can be excruciatingly hard-hitting, however. Tang is not soft on the crucial issues of Christian social ethics. One spot pans across children's emaciated faces for about twenty silent seconds. Then the narrator says: "There are five million hungry children in the United States. You've just met thirty of them."

Another Tang spot, which irritated realtors, featured a young couple being shown a house by a real estate agent. After a positive response to the property, the husband asks:

"Are there any blacks in the neighborhood?"

"Absolutely not!"

"You mean this is a restricted neighborhood?"

"Absolutely!"

"We've changed our minds," the wife replies. Exit the couple.

One of the major problems of religious television spots is that they are by their very nature so short and startling that they virtually require repetition. Commercial advertisers insist as much on saturation by repetition as on prime-time exposure (which is obvious to anyone who has watched television for any length of time). Martin Neeb of Lutheran Television Productions insists that churches simply cannot afford to produce the kind of spots that are good enough to "stand up"—to be attractive, startling, and relevant when repeatedly exposed for saturation of the broadcast market area. In consequence, he insists, even if religious spots get prime time, they will seldom achieve reinforcement of their messages, because the stations will show them only infrequently. Then the spot becomes outdated and must be replaced by another at considerable expense. Neeb's suggestion is that each religious broadcaster pick one *theme* to produce and air for ten years. That, he thinks, would bring the kind of product that would "stand up."[9]

Tang does not seem to be encountering so great a

---

[9]Personal interview with the author.

problem with spot saturation and durability—partly due, no doubt, to the quality of his spots. A Tucson broadcaster called Tang's spots the best public service he had ever seen. One New York television station ran a single Franciscan spot more than forty times.[10]

Tang is unsure of his results. Indeed, if the objective is to increase churchgoing, the effect of spots probably cannot be evaluated. Tang's hope is that the spots can break through and break down religious ignorance, insincerity, and irrelevance. "We're proving to people that the things that they have always believed in have a place in the fibre of everyday life," Tang declares.

His contemporaneity of vision is appropriate in the light of history. The Franciscans were the first to carry the gospel to North America in the sixteenth century. They continue to do so in the twentieth century with imagination and vigor.

Presbyterian Church, US

The Southern Presbyterian Church began religious spot broadcasting three years before the United Presbyterians. The format arose, they admit, not because they were in the vanguard of a broadcasting trend that was to come to full flower nearly a decade later, but merely because they lacked the funds to do anything of greater length. What motivates both Presbyterian denominations to use spots is what motivates all religious broadcasting agencies who do so: the desire to thrust a Christian message into the minds of the maximum audience of those not shaped by God's claims, and to do so with the highest efficiency and at the lowest possible cost.

Bluford Hestir is director of Television, Radio, and Audio Visuals (TRAV) for the Southern Presbyterians. To talk to him is to gain the distinct impression that—despite the successes his denomination has realized with spots—he finds the medium at its best inadequate. Hestir construes his job, ideally, as a teaching job, "but we cannot teach a course in theology in sixty seconds." On the other hand, if

---

[10]Finnigan, *op. cit.*, p. 46.

one does produce a program that could teach theology, but cannot gain air time for it, nothing has been gained. "When we do not pay for the time," Hestir admits, "we are at the mercy of the station. We have to conform to the state of the art and the market."[11]

Conforming to the state of the market means conforming to the commercial motif. For the most part, Hestir says, this entails sixty-second spots. TRAV has experimented with some sixty-second spots that can be divided in the middle to form two thirty-second spots and thus offer the station manager increased versatility. In all, Hestir and TRAV producer Kirk Hammond attempt to keep the nature of the medium in clear focus:

> We are trying to take advantage of the fact that this is a visual medium and that the pictures will tell the story even more than the words. In our "Hot Rod" series, particularly, we use about five to eight words in the entire spot in each case. In one spot we use no words.

When the opportunity presents itself, TRAV has seized the opportunity for specials like "Come Blow Your Horn," the special on jazz in the church discussed above (pp. 99f.). That special did not adopt an overtly didactic format, but its content was specifically focused "to demonstrate to the world . . . how the Christian faith applies to life in our world."

> We must speak out of the Reformed faith's heritage and the history of Presbyterianism. "Come Blow Your Horn" speaks to jazz enthusiasts at the expense of turning off other people. We do this under the assumption that jazz started in the church and it has now come back into the church and here is its story.
>
> We planned a series on Country and Western music and other idioms. Each one is related to the theological content of the music. We did a radio program—and we would like to do it on television—using the Beatles and Johnny Cash. It is a very popular religious program for young people. It asks the question, "What is it all about?" It was snapped up by all the top fifty markets.
>
> This is the theological concern we have: using the music, forms, and idioms of the present moment and disclosing the content and nature of the spiritual quest they imply or assert, and doing it in the context of the Reformed faith. The matters concerning Christ, faith, Christian love, and the like are latent in every one of these items.

---

[11] Personal interview with the author.

The posture of spot religious broadcasters is one of expediency. To say one provocative word in a way that sticks in the human mind is better than to have no chance at all to say many well-chosen words. In Father Libby's words,

> The Golden Rule is not the whole of Christianity any more than "Twinkle, Twinkle, Little Star" is the whole of astronomy. But the Golden Rule is a basic theological and ethical building block. To say that much or that kind of thing well to a major audience is of value.[12]

The claim that religious spots work as leaven is as much hope as fact. Their impact would be extremely difficult, if not impossible, to measure, though the logic of the broadcasters who use them is convincing. In any case, these broadcasters have waged a valiant campaign on a difficult field of battle, and they have done so with wisdom and imagination.

Other Leavening Influences

Some religious broadcasters would contend that there is a far better way than spot broadcasting to make the Word a leaven for godliness in the land. It is the interview of leading churchmen on one of the prime-time commercial variety or dialogue shows. Increasingly, religious broadcasters are undertaking what might be called a ministry *to* broadcasting, in order to get a religious ministry *by* commercial broadcasters, rather than just *through* broadcasting.

Paul Stevens suggests that his documentaries on network prime time really have their main impact as a kind of leaven. The archaeological data of "Zarethan" or the biblical story of "The Vine" lodges in the minds and feelings of the viewers, Stevens claims, and creates a subconscious as well as a conscious disposition in favor of the certainty of the gospel. In a sense, all of the teaching programs in religious broadcasting probably have that same long-range effect.

However, the difference between the confrontation of

---

[12]Personal interview with the author.

humans in the lecture or documentary and that in the interview show and spot is significant. The interview of the Archbishop of Canterbury on the Dick Cavett show has the effect of a live-audience encounter, with a specific problem of godly life or thought, in a situation in which the question can be raised by an "antagonist" and a live witness is forced to address it then and there with his confession of the relevance of his faith.

The United Methodist, United Presbyterian, and Episcopal broadcasting divisions have joined efforts since 1970 to minister to the broadcasting industry by encouraging program hosts like Dick Cavett, David Frost, and Johnny Carson to invite available religious figures to appear. Leading religious persons of international repute are constantly moving through New York and Hollywood and can conveniently be scheduled for a taping on regular network programs. Frequently the "Today Show" features such figures as well, and occasionally major newscasters will interview leading churchmen. The exposure is usually a significant length of time to a prime-time audience, and it costs the religious community nothing, since it is regular commercial broadcasting. The value to the show itself, in terms of relevance and audience appeal, is usually very great. The service this provides the church and the religious community is incomparable.

This approach of helping the broadcasting industry create its own religious ministry is being given increasing priority by religious broadcasters. Everett Parker insists that it should be the primary, if not exclusive, function of religious broadcast agencies and staffs, claiming—with considerable persuasiveness—that the networks and stations have a responsibility to the religious community to air programs suited to their needs, as well as to those of all other segments of the population.[13]

Father Libby of the Episcopal Church records some successes in this type of endeavor:

> We had the Archbishop of Canterbury and Cardinal Suenens on the "Today Show" and on David Frost and Dick Cavett. We did a full-scale press conference covered by everyone of the networks

---

[13] See Chapter 7 for a further elaboration of Parker's struggle against current industry standards and practices.

and all the local stations. CBS filmed a joint lecture these two men gave ... and presented it as a thirty-minute program. Obviously, we got much more effect from that than from putting an equivalent of our own production effort and money into an equivalent amount of air time.

The best were the Frost and Cavett shows, where the Archbishop appeared with Jane Fonda. Jane proceeded to attack him. He handled the matter very well. He was intrigued with her life and work.[14]

In addition, such lesser-known national programs as David Susskind's broadcasts have featured religious leaders or discussions on spiritual, moral, and theological problems relevant to America today. Local specialists in fermenting confrontations, like Lou Gordon of Detroit, frequently deal with spiritual issues and churchmen of note or notoriety.

In addition, it is often possible to achieve the Ramsey-Fonda kind of confrontation in regular network religious shows. In June 1970, "Lamp Unto My Feet," the CBS weekly broadcast, featured China historian George Carothers and David Stout of the Division of Overseas Ministries of the NCC, a former missionary in China. Stout is a real China expert and engaged in discussion with Carothers about China's future. June 1970 was crucial timing in relationship to the consequences of the "Cultural Revolution" going on at that time. It was a fascinating discussion that ranged over such issues as the moral and ethical motivations of Chairman Mao. At a time prior to the relaxing of Sino-American tensions, it was particularly illuminating for the American people.[15]

Of similar character were Paul Stevens' hour-long interviews with leading religious figures like Malcolm Muggeridge, which appeared several times on ABC's "Directions." Muggeridge's conversations with Stevens, under the title "Crisis or Chaos," confronted present-day Americans with crucial issues of spiritual and moral responsibility in a way and with an authority that must have forced the ideas to continue to ferment in the minds of viewers for some considerable time.

[14]Personal interview with the author.
[15]Personal conversation between the author and Everett C. Parker.

MODELS OF RELIGIOUS BROADCASTING

The dialogue format is a particularly potent spiritual and social leaven technique. The Detroit Council of Churches has employed it on a regular basis for many years. Channel 7 in Detroit has run "Dialogue" weekly for eleven years. This half-hour ecumenical show is normally hosted by a Protestant pastor and a Catholic priest, and frequently features additional guests. Currently it is hosted by Father Edward Baldwin, director of the National Vocations Office under the National Board of Catholic Bishops of Washington, D.C., and the present author. Channel 2 carries a similar program at a more desirable time, called "Let's See," also moderated by the present author. It has featured leading churchmen in dialogue.

The effectiveness of dialogue for social and spiritual leavening is rooted in its very nature. Religious dialogue sets about mainly to raise the crucial questions of responsible godliness. It assumes that the urgent need is to get the questions clearly focused and defined. Once that is achieved, directions may be suggested for pursuing the answers, but the pursuit is largely left to the motivation and quest of the audience.

Precisely this intent is behind religious spots. They produce leavening ferment by raising the crucial questions, not by imposing the answers. The technique is obviously a teaching technique primarily, and one that is as old as Socrates. It is designed to incite growth and maturity, not dogmatism and conformity. It assumes that with the correct stimulation such growth can be spiritual and moral healing and redemption.

To try to predict the future is to risk being proved wrong. Whether the leaven of spots and dialogue will be the model for religious broadcasting of the 1970s, or whether, as Larry McMaster predicts,[16] the leaven will come from a renaissance of the dramatic and documentary formats, is difficult to predict. Christian broadcasters will, in any case, have to face the future with vision and faith.

Two things about that future seem clear. First, society will move at an increasing rather than a decreasing pace, giving even more growing room to the potential for inhu-

---

[16]Personal interview with the author.

manity that arises when societies lose time for people. Thus, broadcasters will have to find ways to address people with less rational cerebration, shorter attention spans, more ephemeral values, greater superficiality, and deeper isolation from each other. Second, the citizens of Western society will be just as greatly in need of instruction, forgiveness, profound insight, and assurance of the meaning and purpose of their lives and relationships as humans have ever been. The need for communication—especially the communication of the Christian gospel—will be greater than ever before, since humans will tend to be more alienated and less responsible than ever before. The task of communication will be more formidable because humans will be more mobile, less given to reflective rationality, and preoccupied with today's wages, not eternal verities.

Spots, interviews, life-situation drama, and documentaries may not teach much theology well. But they may be the only chance. We may have to exploit their every potential. And perhaps they will pay off as the leaven whose insertion into the "body politic" leavens the whole. The quality of the leaven will, of course, be crucial. It may well make the difference between spiritual and moral vigor and starvation.

seven

The Failed Promise

Parker's Fight

Everett C. Parker is director of the Office of Communication for the United Church of Christ. For many years he has been chairman of the Broadcasting and Film Commission of the National Council of Churches. He is, without question, one of the most aggressive, imaginative, and concerned figures in religious broadcasting today. His insight, imagination, and courage have illuminated the history of religious broadcasting in America since World War II.

In the mid-1940s Parker was a prime mover in the establishment of the JRRC, which broke up the marriage of the networks to the Federal Council of Churches. He was influential in encouraging independent denominational programming nationwide in the late 1940s. He was, in the early 1950s, singularly responsible for creative ferment

THE FAILED PROMISE

about what varieties of format are suited to the broadcast media. He was instrumental in the production of some of the most imaginative religious broadcasting in the late 1950s and the 1960s. He has written three major books about religious radio and television broadcasting and audience impact.[1]

In recent years Parker has turned to a wholly new prophetic role in religious broadcasting—a crusade for ethical integrity in mass media communication. Parker's fight has taken the very tangible course of refusing to produce religious programming for radio and television. He has called for a strike against the industry, in which religious broadcasters would withhold their programming from commercial broadcasters. His rationale and objectives are clear and simple:

> We are opposed to broadcast programming... because of the treatment which the industry gives to religious programming. Religion is greatly discriminated against by the television and radio industry.... I think that we [the NCC] ought to pull out of our network relationship and let them, if they wish, do their religious broadcasting when everybody is asleep or in church or busy with their meals. But we should fight with them and not cooperate with them. We should not provide them our resources.[2]

Parker's last broadcast effort was the 1968 production "Tangled World," Roger Shinn's "seminary course in Christian ethics" for adults. Since then his time and energy have been exhausted not in talk about ethics, or programs regarding ethics, but in trying to create an ethical world in broadcasting. The battle has many fronts. It involves first of all attacks on racial discrimination in broadcasting.[3] Parker has successfully sued stations on behalf of misused minority persons. Since the merger that formed the United Church of Christ in 1957, it has aimed in its mass communications efforts to awaken the public to the dangers in the misuse of television and radio. Combined with the denom-

---

[1] *The Television-Radio Audience and Religion* (with David W. Barry and Dallas W. Smythe, 1955); *Religious Radio* (1957); and *Religious Television* (1961).

[2] Personal interview with the author.

[3] Cf. Ralph M. Jennings, *How to Protect Citizens' Rights in Television and Radio*, p. 4; published by the United Church of Christ.

ination's concern for racial justice, this has spawned efforts to establish the rights of black Americans to the services of the media. Parker wrote in 1968:

> The stations in Jackson, Mississippi, where 47 per cent of the population is black, were particularly contemptuous of black concerns. In 1964, the United Church monitored these stations, and then petitioned the FCC not to renew their licenses, on the grounds that they had deprived blacks of the proper enjoyment of broadcasting facilities, given a distorted picture of vital issues, discriminated against blacks in various ways, and—particularly in the case of station WLBT-TV—had advocated resistance to integration laws.[4]

A second kind of discrimination against which Parker has taken successful legal action is the broadcasters' bias, bolstered by the Federal Communications Commission, against distinctive program content:

> By keeping the public out of its affairs, the Federal Communications Commission kept the industry protected from anybody making any judgment on the broadcaster's performance. We went to circuit court and got the WLBT decision, which gave standing to the public *vis-à-vis* the broadcasting industry. This opened the door for the people to say that we are going to have what we want on the air, not what broadcasters want to give us—what broadcasters are trying to unload on us for their private profit.[5]

At stake in Parker's fight is the opportunity for the church to influence our culture significantly and shape its values. As Martin Marty has asserted, the authenticity of the church implies an intimate involvement with the social and cultural context in which the church lives.[6] Parker is serious about gaining that type of involvement for the church. He is increasingly impatient with the church's compromising and yielding to the temptation to conform and get along in broadcasting.

Mere appeals to conscience are not particularly effective in dealing with the industry and trying to force it to allow the church a more satisfactory access to the media. Fortunately, the cause for which Parker is fighting is rooted in

---

[4]Everett C. Parker, "The Ethics of Mass Communication Practices," in *Access to the Air*, p. 17.
[5]Personal interview with the author.
[6]Cf. Martin E. Marty, *The Improper Opinion*.

the history of broadcasting legislation, which gives him access to the weapon of law. Broadcasters are licensed, and thus subject to the control of the people, *if the people are willing to exercise that control.*

The Radio Act of 1912 laid the legislative foundation for broadcasting law in the United States. The Radio Act of 1927 fleshed out that law, established detailed procedures for licensing broadcasters, and set up the Federal Radio Commission, forerunner of the Federal Communications Commission. It also specified that all broadcasting must be in the "public convenience, interest, or necessity."[7] The Communications Act of 1934 reinforced the legal point that the airways are, in fact, natural resources. Broadcasters may be licensed to exploit the potentials of the airways, even for profit, but what they broadcast must be primarily "in the public interest." The "Mayflower Doctrine" of 1941 established that a broadcaster, as a licensee of the people, may not be an advocate, but must present both sides of an issue with equal time, serving the legitimate needs of all segments of the public with both his commercial programs and his public service time.[8] Considerable subsequent legislation has expanded the law, all of it reinforcing Parker's central point: the broadcaster exists for the public interest.

If the industry leaders can be compelled by legal or moral means "to hire minorities; give *in-depth* coverage of political problems; and sacrifice some profit so that the American people will be better able to understand the true picture of life in this society, be better informed, and be better able to make up their own minds,"[9] Parker believes the religious community will also be able to get prime broadcast time. In no sense does he endorse second-rate religious programs. But finding religious programming of competitive quality with commercial programming is not the problem, as he sees it. There is plenty of great religious programming. Few see it, however, because it is either not

---

[7]Barnouw, *A Tower in Babel*, p. 301.
[8]Barnouw, *The Golden Web*, pp. 226, 259.
[9]Personal interview with the author.

accepted by the broadcasters, relegated to useless time, or not even produced and distributed because the church cannot afford to do so.

Parker argues that the "fairness doctrine," despite its ring of solid liberal principles of democracy, is used by broadcasters to keep good religious broadcasting off the air. The doctrine gives them an excuse to lean heavily toward representative agencies like the NCC as the source of religious programs. Since the NCC wants to keep the broadcasters happy and since it represents many different churches, it is disinclined to distinctive and prophetic broadcasting. Church agencies who would broadcast prophetically find that the public service time has already been allocated to the NCC. They are generally unable, for financial reasons, to buy time on the air, so the broadcasters, asserts Parker, have essentially kept hard-hitting religious broadcasting off the air.[10]

Parker's criticism on this point is somewhat exaggerated. NCC broadcasting (as he himself will admit—and largely because of his leadership) is *often* distinctive and prophetic. Furthermore, the wide variety of the religious broadcasters served by the NCC should not be overlooked. Moreover, a number of independents (like the Christian Reformed Church in radio and the Church of Christ in television) do succeed in purchasing time for national broadcasts.

In any case it is clear to Parker that the health of the American culture, the religious community, and the climate of real democracy in broadcasting are at stake in this issue. That means further that the broadcasters are not only responsible to provide religious broadcasters with good public service time slots. It requires extended public service segments in prime time. Most of all, it requires, in Parker's judgment, that the broadcasters pay production and distribution costs for religious programs, as they do for public service news shows, community charities shows, and shows of nonprofit organizations.

As long as the church is at the mercy of the broadcast

---

[10] On the fairness doctrine, see Kenneth A. Cox, "The Fairness Doctrine and Its Challengers," in *Access to the Air*, pp. 12ff.

industry in her efforts at religious use of the mass media it is obvious that she cannot be true to herself. Parker's fight and Parker's posture in broadcasting is a crucial theological and ethical issue. The particular importance of the fight is captured in Martin Marty's words:

> If we could honestly claim that we have made a first step in effectively encountering the world that is spellbound by the public media, we could dismiss the subject with a bored smile. Such luxury is not granted us.[11]

Morality in Media

Parker's fight involves another controversial question raised by the mass media: the problem of sexual immorality, vulgar language, and violence over the public airways. Parker is against all of them. Most Americans discuss media morality vigorously. Few are in a position to do much about it except for occasional participation in letter-writing campaigns. Parker can and does do something about it. For the last decade he has promoted a campaign to make the government—through the FCC—concerned to take action that will insure responsible broadcasting without censorship and commercial morality without prudish coercion.

This dimension of Parker's fight has not been without its effect on government figures. Already in 1966 Senator John Pastore made a major speech on sex and violence in broadcasting to an assembly of women executives in the broadcast industry. He spoke with his usual candor and vigor:

> How long can we rifle through the files of the studios for decent pictures... before we hit the bottom of the barrel? Will the industry retreat from its public responsibility and descend... to "Divorce-Italian Style" and "Never On Sunday?"

Commenting on Pastore's speech only six years later Max Gunther put the current state of the issue in focus.

> The two films he mentioned have already appeared on TV and today are considered charmingly modest, if not actually quaint. Compared with some other entertainments that have turned up

[11]Marty, *op. cit.*, p. 18.

on TV in the past year or two, and will appear in the coming months, the two films that so outraged Senator Pastore seem hardly more daring than a Mickey Mouse cartoon.

Startled viewers have seen explicitly sexy movies such as "A Man and a Woman," "The Anderson Tapes," and "The Damned." Films such as "Patton," complete with strong language that once would have been edited out, will appear this season, as will dramas dealing with such once-taboo subjects as homosexuality. Full frontal nudity has turned up on stations of the Public Broadcasting System and seems no more than a year or two away in commercial programming. Topics such as lesbianism are freely discussed on talk shows, while comedy shows feature humor that a 1966 audience would have considered improper outside a stag party. Daytime soap operas deal frankly with adultery and even show unmarried couples in bed together.[12]

The issue is not a simple one. Even stating the problem precisely is difficult. Is nudity immoral? Of course not. Is realism in communication arts evil because it is sometimes disgusting? Obviously not. How far may Christians seek to impose their standards on others? Must the pornography seeker be regulated by the same standards as the parent who wishes to control the environment of his child?[13] These are difficult questions that have engaged the attention of sincere and thoughtful Christians for a long time without achieving a clear-cut and satisfactory resolution. The religious moralist, cited by Gunther, who insists that the TV set is no longer a welcome guest in his home and asserts, "I would no more plug it in today than I would invite a prostitute to dinner," may think the answer is simple, but he does so only because he does not grasp the nature of the questions.

On the other hand, responsibility to the public interest cannot simply be set aside by insisting that those who oppose the prurient character of pornography are prudes. One facet of the decisions to be made will surely be what is appropriate in view of the makeup of the local and national audience at various times of day. Frank sexual

---

[12]Max Gunther, "TV and the New Morality," *TV Guide*, Oct. 14, 1972.

[13]Lewis B. Smedes, "Prudery and Pornography," *The Reformed Journal*, Sept. 1973, p. 4.

discussion, for example, in an honest and otherwise worthy television program may have one value at 4:00 p.m. when the predominant audience is children and quite another value at 11:30 p.m. when most children are asleep. Another consideration—which should not be overemphasized, to be sure—is that local stations can select what network fare they wish to broadcast and individual viewers can exercise the ultimate censorship of the on-off switch and the channel selector.

Lawrence Carino, general manager of WJBK, the CBS affiliate in Detroit, is a committed Catholic Christian, who describes himself as a believer in "traditional moral values." He schedules movies from a variety of non-network sources whenever he feels the network feature is inappropriate for his audience. Carino insists that the new morality is the same as the old immorality. Whether he is right or wrong about that—and about his particular judgments—he has nonetheless demonstrated that local stations are free to exercise personal moral judgment in terms of the needs and interests of their communities.

The Challenge

The question of morality in media is far more important, however, than would be suggested by those who limit their concern to sex and violence. The loss of cultural idealism in radio and television today may prove, in the long run, infinitely more serious and degrading. The mass media have become potent arbiters of value in our society, and the cultural and spiritual idealism they communicate will eventually shape our culture and society. In the final analysis, humans become in large part what they are taught to digest and/or confess.

> The media, if they are truly *mass* media, set out to shape in men "the proper opinions," to make them common men and women, unknown citizens somehow at the mercy of the communicator. Because of the hours of attention they command and the apparent quality that is theirs owing to the economic potential, they usually achieve this aim. It is in such a world that Christianity makes its claim and its offer. It presents a paradox, a foolishness,

something "contrary to the opinion." It has an Improper Opinion for the Uncommon Man: for the known citizen of the commonwealth whose builder and maker is God.[14]

Motivated by similar conviction, Parker has repeatedly called for intensive review of station license renewals and public service performance. He has urged enforcement on networks and stations alike of the provision that broadcasting must be in the public interest. No one concerned with how the minds and wills of people are being molded can ignore the mass media. They will inevitably influence how Christianity will be imaged, shaped, viewed, and understood in the next century. That, in turn, will determine what influence Christianity will have.[15] It was an exaggerated euphoria that led the church of the 1950s to expect radio and television to provide the panacea of mass evangelism. It may not be an exaggerated despair in the 1970s to suggest that the character of the mass media and their secularizing cultural consequences may make the church's mission thoroughly impossible very soon.

There is an intense competition between the forces pursuing the spirits of men. Mass media are significant because they can compete more powerfully on behalf of the ideologies they represent than can books, sermons, or Scripture. And what ideology do the mass media represent? Their values are commodity-centered, keyed to the need of mass production industries for mass consumption markets.

Over and over mass communication dins into our ears and unrolls before our eyes the four myths of hedonistic, mass-structured society:

1. History is progress (we are getting better and better).
2. Happiness is the chief end of life.
3. Man is basically good.
4. Ultimately, material things are *every*thing.

Through mass communication we are conditioned to look upon ourselves primarily as consumers and everything else is made to appear as a commodity that can be bartered and consumed. . . .

---

[14]Marty, *op. cit.*, p. 32.
[15]On this, see Everett C. Parker, "Christian Communication and Secular Man," and Kenneth Cox, "The FCC, The Churches, and Public Responsibility in Broadcasting."

THE FAILED PROMISE

The Psalmist asks: "What is man?" Mass communication has the answer: Man is a consumer. But the consumer is a prime example of the isolated self, glorying in self-gratification. Religion denies that this pursuit of self-gratification can account adequately for the sources of human action and human satisfaction. Yet religion, too, is looked upon as a commodity, something that can be packaged attractively and labelled and sold for the service it can render in helping you to attain success, happiness, social adjustment, and similar transitory desires. How many times do we hear even good church members insist that the church, like everybody else, has something to sell? Its product is "religion."[16]

What can the church do? She must use her power to require broadcasters to be responsible to the ideals of a wholesome society, culture, faith, and hope for humanity.[17] Cultural idealism is not outmoded. Christian objectives are relevant as ever. Spiritual health is as central a need, as profound a longing, as devastating a hunger, and as redemptive a possibility for twentieth-century Americans as it was for first-century Greeks, Romans, and Jews. Presumably that is what Marty means:

> The retreat of the churches, the rollback of their empires, the withdrawal of their claims, the slackening of their hold on people is sufficiently marked to make the entire world—including the West—missionary territory. Words written or spoken, images formed, hopes made incandescent in such a time, are worthless and wasted if they do not keep this reconciling purpose in view.
>
> The reconciling message of God's activity in Jesus Christ is the same from age to age. It has outlasted and sometimes outwitted competition in other times and other places. It would be heard again by people in need in this age of mass media and mass men.[18]

Harvey Cox registers a similar concern in his recent book, *The Seduction of the Spirit*. He argues that radio and television are not neutral media, no matter what the fairness doctrine and Mayflower doctrine require. The broadcaster, prohibited from advocacy, tends to a common-denominator kind of program, which turns out, says Cox, to reduce all values to what will sell most effectively. And that is programming which appeals to the

---

[16] Parker, "Christian Communication and Secular Man."
[17] See Everett C. Parker and Lawrence M. Carino, "Human Rights in the World of Broadcasting."
[18] Marty, *op. cit.*, p. 15.

most crass and animalistic and the least idealistic in humans.

The cultural and spiritual tragedy is that broadcasters, in trying to avoid advocacy, advocate the belief that cultural idealism is not real, sensible, or chic. The result is a "broadcast gospel" of secularism and debased materialistic humanism. Nicholas Johnson, recently retired commissioner of the Federal Communications Commission, and author of *How To Talk Back to Your Television Set*, endorsed Cox's point.

> I have become more and more aware of the extent to which television not only distributes programs and sells products, but also preaches a general philosophy of life.... Many products (and even programs)... sell the gospel that there are instant solutions to life's most pressing personal problems. You don't need to think about your own emotional maturity and development of individuality, your discipline, training, and education, your willingness, to cooperate and compromise and work with other people; you don't need to think about developing deep and meaningful human relationships and trying to keep them in repair.[19]

In discussing humanness as an alternative to this crass consumerism, Johnson observes that the broadcasting industry—and traditional religious broadcasting—contributes virtually nothing to "life, liberty and the pursuit of happiness." If he is correct—and who will challenge him—where has government gone? It was once thought to be the government's business to guarantee the opportunity for those three rights. Since the government, through the FCC, regulates the use of airways, why is no action taken to put humanness and humaneness back into broadcast programming?

No one disputes human vulnerability to conditioning and manipulation by appeals to our appetites. But our mere vulnerability does not mean that we all idealize those appetites above healthy spirituality or cultural idealism. Any honest human being will admit that he needs all the help he can get to find his way to cultural, religious, spiritual, and moral growth and health. Since that is so, manipulation by commercial appeals to greed, competi-

---

[19]Nicholas Johnson, "The Careening of America," *The Humanist*, July/Aug. 1972, p. 11.

tion, possession of objects, and the like is the crassest and most immoral kind of exploitation and enslavement of the populace.

Most broadcasters will claim, of course, that they produce only the programs that people really want. The Nielsen ratings, they will argue, are the most important determinant for programming, and these ratings prove what people really watch. Such logic is erroneous to the point of hilarity. First of all, the rating systems currently available are all prejudicial in terms of the value categories and data collection techniques they employ. Second, the rating systems provide no method for registering specialized audience tastes. Third, the ratings do not offer the viewer the chance to register a judgment for or against a program that is never shown but might conceivably be developed in an attractive fashion for the public.

There is a good deal of evidence to suggest that Americans today are under personal and social stresses and strains unknown in the past. This derives in part from the consumerist life-style that broadcasting promotes in the place of growth, individuality, and wholesome alternative life-styles. Johnson thinks there is some evidence that Americans are beginning to rebel, casting aside those standards, and demanding more humanness and creativity for their lives. That seems too optimistic, though it is a marvelous possibility. Considering the potential for self-discipline of consumers, illustrated when public recognition was first given to the energy crisis, it may be true that Americans are arriving at the point where quality is becoming a higher priority than conformity.

Cox is less optimistic. He claims that while many are turning to spiritual, cultural, religious, and moral values today, most youth have already been captured by a new religion—the television fantasy world. He contends that the frenzied consumerism of American broadcasting has shaped the morals and ideals of the whole Western world. He pleads for a "theological response to the challenge of the mass media."

> Our dilemma is a serious one. Cut off by the currents of the age both from my own inner story and from the story of my people, I listen for another story to hear and to tell myself. I listen because I have no real choice.

As a homo sapiens, I am an incorrigibly story-telling animal. Literally, I cannot live without a story. But I do not have to search long. A substitute is readily supplied. The most powerful technologies ever devised churn out signals to keep me pliable, immature and weak. They hit at my most vulnerable spot. There is still time for us to learn again to tell stories—mine, yours, ours. If we do not, the signals will sweep all before them. Their gentle bleeps and reassuring winks will lull us into a trance from which there is no awakening. If there is any hell where souls are lost forever, that would be it.[20]

What theological alternatives exist? The answer is not simply to say that it is the church's task to defend and interpret Christianity and its institution against so massive an insult. "Christianity is obligated by faith to defend man himself against belittlements, attacks. The church's task is to be the advocate of man, especially where man is weak, poor or powerless."[21] That, of course, has been Parker's point since 1946. It is encouraging that the band of champions for that view is growing.

No significant improvement seems likely unless the recognition is widespread that the current "state of the art" of the broadcast industry is menace not just to religion but to human dignity, authenticity, and integrity. Unfortunately, religion and religious broadcasters have long been far too ready to accept sops from the industry as bribes to prevent the airing of prophetic and distinctive programming that champions man. Much religious programming championed man as the dignified son of God, but who has seen it? How profoundly and intensively was it allowed to teach? Parker has put his finger on the essential point. The problem is not primarily the quality of religious programs, but the complete inability of religious broadcasters to influence the shape and quality of all the commercial programming that goes on in prime and near-prime time.

Parker's fight goes on. It is a long way from won. The battlefield is not even clearly delineated. The strategy is certainly not obvious. The logistics are likely to be formidably expensive. But the matter at stake is, in many ways, an issue of spiritual life or death for America.

[20] Harvey Cox, "Is TV Seducing Our Souls?", *The Sunday News Magazine of The Detroit News*, Sept. 23, 1973, pp. 25, 28.
[21] *Ibid.*

Bibliography

Books

A Communications Manual for Judicatories of the Church. New York: Division of Mass Media of the United Presbyterian Church in the United States of America, 1958.

Access to the Air. New York: Graduate School of Journalism, Columbia University, 1968.

Adams, J. C.; Carpenter, C. R.; and D. H. Smith. *College Teaching by Television.* Washington, D.C.: American Council on Education, 1958.

Allen, Louise C., and others. *Radio and Television Continuity Writing.* New York: Pitman, 1962.

Annual of the Southern Baptist Convention, 1938, 1942, and 1947. Nashville: Southern Baptist Convention, 1938, 1942, and 1947.

Annual Report, 1931. New York: Federal Council of Churches, 1932.

Arons, Leon, and Mark A. May, eds. *Television and Human Behavior: Tomorrow's Research in Mass Communication.* New York: Appleton-Century-Crofts, 1963.

Ashley, Paul P. *"Say It Simply": Legal Limits in Publishing, Radio*

and Television. Seattle and Lonio: University of Washington, 1965.
Augenstein, Leroy. *Come Let Us Play God.* New York: Harper and Row, 1969.
Bachman, John W. *The Church in the World of Radio-Television.* New York: Association Press, 1960.
Bannister, Harry. *The Education of a Broadcaster.* New York: Simon and Schuster, 1965.
Barnouw, Erik. *The Golden Web.* New York: Oxford U. P., 1968.
———. *The Image Empire.* New York: Oxford U. P., 1970.
———. *Mass Communication.* New York and Toronto: Holt, Rinehart and Winston, 1965.
———. *The Television Writer.* New York: Hill and Wang, 1962.
———. *A Tower in Babel.* New York: Oxford U. P., 1966.
Batchelor, C. D. *Communication: From Cave Writing to Television.* New York: Harcourt, Brace, 1953.
Becker, Samuel, and H. Clay Harshbarger. *Television: Techniques for Planning and Performance.* New York: Holt, 1958.
Berelson, Bernard. *Content Analysis in Communication Research.* Glencoe, Ill.: The Free Press, 1952.
Berlo, David K. *The Process of Communication.* New York: Holt, Rinehart and Winston, 1960.
Biennial Report, 1936, 1946. New York: Federal Council of Churches of Christ, 1937, 1947.
Bluem, A. William. *Documentary in American Television.* New York: Hastings House, 1964.
———. *Religious Television Programs, A Study of Relevance.* New York: Hastings House, 1969.
———. *Television in the Public Interest.* New York: Hastings House, 1961.
———. *Television—The Creative Experience.* New York: Hastings House, 1967.
Board of Christian Education of the United Presbyterian Church. *Viewers' Guide for Man and His Problems.* New York: National Council of Churches of Christ, 1961.
Bogart, Leo. *The Age of Television.* New York: Ungar, 1967.
Bormann, Ernest. *Theory and Research in the Communication Arts.* New York: Holt, Rinehart and Winston, 1965.
Brackbill, Charles, Jr.; Stockford, Donald; Barrett, Donald; Price, Nelson; and Bonnie Brennan. *Report of Task Force on Communications.* New York: National Conference of Christian Broadcasters, 1969.
Bradley, William L. *The Meaning of Christian Values Today.* Philadelphia: Westminster (Westminster Studies in Christian Communication Series), 1964.
Bretz, Rudy. *Techniques of Television Production.* New York: McGraw-Hill, 1962.
Bretz, Rudy, and Edward Stafheff. *Television Program—Its Direction and Production.* New York: Hill and Wang, 1962.

BIBLIOGRAPHY

Bryson, Lyman, ed. *The Communication of Ideas.* New York: Cooper Square, 1964.
Bussell, J. *The Art of Television.* London: Faber and Faber.
Carnegie Commission. *Public Television, A Program for Action.* New York: Bantam, 1967.
Cherry, Colin. *On Human Communication.* Cambridge, Mass.: M.I.T. Press, 1957.
Chester, G.; Garnett, G. P.; and E. E. Willis. *Television and Radio* (3rd ed.). New York: Appleton-Century-Crofts, 1963.
A Communication Manual for Judicatories of the Church. New York: Division of Mass Media of the UPUSA, 1958.
Coons, John E., ed. *Freedom and Responsibility in Broadcasting.* Evanston: Northwestern University, 1961.
Costillo, L., and G. Gordon. *Teach with Television.* New York: Hastings House, 1961.
Cox, Harvey. *The Seduction of the Spirit.* New York: Simon and Schuster, 1973.
Crowley, Thomas. *Modern Communication.* New York: Columbia University, 1961.

Dale, Edgar. *Audio-Visual Methods in Teaching.* New York: Dryden, 1966.
Department of Research and Education of the Federal Council of Churches of Christ. *Broadcasting and the Public.* New York: Abingdon, 1938.
Dewey, John. *Art as Experience.* Putnam's, 1959.
_____. *Philosophy of Education.* Ames, Iowa: Littlefield, Adams, 1956.
Dizard, Wilson P. *Television: A World View.* Syracuse: Syracuse University, 1966.
Dow, C. W., ed. *Introduction to Graduate Study in Speech and Theatre.* East Lansing, Mich.: Michigan State University, 1961.

Edgar, Earl E. *Social Foundations of Education.* New York: The Center for Applied Research in Education, 1965.
Eisenstein, Sergei. *Film Form.* New York: Harcourt, Brace and World, 1969.
_____. *Film Form and the Film Sense.* New York: Meridian (World), 1969.
Eisenson, Jon, and others. *The Psychology of Communication.* New York: Appleton-Century-Crofts, 1963.
Eldersveld, Peter H. *Nothing but the Gospel.* Grand Rapids: Eerdmans, 1966.
Emery, E.; Ault, O. H.; and W. K. Agee. *Introduction to Mass Communication* (2nd ed.). New York and Toronto: Dodd, Mead, 1965.
Emery, Walter B. *Broadcasting and Government.* East Lansing, Mich.: Michigan State University, 1961.

Fagal, William A. *By Faith I Live.*

Field, Stanley. *Television and Radio Writing.* Boston: Houghton Mifflin, 1958.
Friendly, Fred W. *Due to Circumstances Beyond Our Control.* New York: Random House, 1967.

Gilbert, Richard R. *Theological Implications for Broadcasting.* New York: The Division of Mass Media, 1966.
Gombrich, Ernest. *Art and Illusion.* New York: Pantheon, 1961.
Gordon, George N. *Educational Television.* New York: The Center for Applied Research in Education, 1965.
Gordon, G. N.; Falk, I.; and W. Hodapp. *The Idea Invaders.* New York: Hastings House, 1963.
Gordon, G. N., and I. Falk. *On-the-Spot Reporting: Radio Records History.* New York: Messner, 1967.
Gottschalk, L. *Understanding History.* New York: Knopf, 1950.
Greene, Robert S. *Television Writing.* New York: Harper, 1956.
Griswold, Clayton T., and Charles H. Schmitz. *How You Can Broadcast Religion.* New York: National Council of Churches of Christ, 1957.
Gulley, Halbert E. *Discussion, Conference, and Group Process.* New York: Holt, Rinehart and Winston, 1960.

Hall, S., and P. Whannel. *The Popular Arts.* New York: Pantheon, 1965.
Harlow, A. F. *Old Wires and New Waves.* New York: Appleton-Century, 1936.
Harwell, Robert Lee. *Fish for My People.* New York: Morehouse-Barlow, 1968.
Hazard, P. D., ed. *TV as Art.* Champaign, Ill.: National Council of Teachers of English, 1966.
Head, Sidney W. *Broadcasting in America.* New York: Houghton Mifflin, 1956.
Herman, Lewis. *A Practical Manual of Screen Playwriting for Theatre and Television Films.* Cleveland and New York: World, 1952.
Hilliard, R. L. *Radio Broadcasting.* New York: Hastings House, 1967.
———. *Understanding Television.* New York: Hastings House, 1964.
———. *Writing for Television and Radio.* New York: Hastings House, 1962.
Hodapp, W. *The Television Actor's Manual.* New York: Appleton-Century-Crofts, 1955.
How To Protect Citizen Rights in Television and Radio. New York: Office of Communications of the United Church of Christ, 1968.
Hyde, Stuart W. *Television and Radio Announcing.* New York: Houghton Mifflin, 1959.

Jackson, B. R., Jr., ed. *Communication-Learning for Churchmen.* Nashville: Abingdon, 1968.
Jocquet, Constant H., Jr., ed. *Yearbook of American Churches.* New York: Council Press, 1970.

BIBLIOGRAPHY

Katz, Elihu, and Paul F. Lazarsfeld. *Personal Influence: The Part Played by People in the Flow of Mass Communication.* Glencoe, Ill.: The Free Press, 1955.
Kaufman, William T. *How To Direct for Television.* New York: Hastings House, 1962.
Kingston, Walter K., and R. Cowgill. *Television Acting and Directing.* New York: Holt, Rinehart and Winston, 1965.
Klapper, Joseph T. *The Effects of Mass Communication.* New York: Free Press, 1960.
Koestler, Arthur. *The Act of Creation.* New York: Dell, 1966.
Kraemer, Hendrick. *The Communication of the Christian Faith.* Philadelphia: Westminster, 1956.
Kuhns, William. *The Electronic Gospel.* New York: Herder and Herder, 1969.

Lacy, Dan. *Freedom and Communications.* Urbana, Ill.: University of Illinois, 1961.
Lawson, John Howard. *Film, The Creative Process.* New York: Hill and Wang, 1964.
Lawton, S. P. *The Modern Broadcaster.* New York: Harper and Brothers, 1961.
Leighton, Isabel, ed. *The Aspirin Age, 1919-41.* New York: Simon and Schuster, 1949.

Maier, Paul L. *A Man Spoke, A World Listened.* New York: McGraw-Hill, 1963.
Marty, Martin E. *The Improper Opinion.* Philadelphia: Westminster (Westminster Studies in Christian Communication Series), 1961.
McLaughlin, W. G., Jr. *Billy Graham: Revivalist in a Secular Age.* New York: Ronald Press, 1960.
McLuhan, Marshall. *The Medium Is the Massage.* New York: Bantam, 1970.
_____ *Understanding Media: The Extensions of Man.* New York: McGraw-Hill, 1964.
McMahon, Harry Wayne. *Television Production.* New York: Hastings House, 1957.
Mehling, H. *The Great Time-Killer.* Cleveland and New York: World, 1962.
Millerson, Gerald. *The Techniques of Television Production.* New York: Hastings House, 1962.
Minow, Newton, and Lawrence Laurent. *Equal Time: The Private Broadcaster and The Public Interest.* New York: Atheneum, 1964.
Mugglebee, Ruth. *Father Coughlin of the Shrine of the Little Flower.* Garden City, N. Y.: Garden City Publishing Company, 1933.
Mulholland, John, and G. N. Gordon. *The Magical Mind.* New York: Hastings House, 1966.

Nathan, Walter L. *Art and the Message of the Church.* Philadelphia: Westminster (Westminster Studies in Christian Communication Series), 1961.

MODELS OF RELIGIOUS BROADCASTING

Noonan, D. P. *The Passion of Fulton Sheen.* New York: Dodd, Mead, 1972.

Ogden, Ward B. *The Television Business.* New York: Ronald Press, 1961.

Parker, Everett C. *Religious Radio.* New York: Harper, 1957.
_____. *Religious Television.* New York: Harper and Brothers, 1961.
Parker, E. C.; Barry, D. W.; and D. W. Smythe. *The Television-Radio Audience and Religion.* New York: Harper and Brothers, 1955.
Peterson, Theodore; Jensen, Jay W.; and William L. Rivers. *The Mass Media and Modern Society.* New York: Holt, Rinehart, and Winston, 1965.
Pollack, John. *Billy Graham.* New York: McGraw-Hill, 1966.

Radio and TV Commission. "Trendex: Special Report, Survey of Religious Program Audiences." Rochester: Archdiocese of New York.
Riesman, David; Glazer, Nathan; and Reuel Denney. *The Lonely Crowd: A Study of the Changing American Character.* Garden City: Doubleday, 1953.
Roberts, Oral. *The Call: An Autobiography.* New York: Doubleday, 1972.
_____. *The Miracle of ORU.* Tulsa: O.R.E.A., 1972.
_____. *My Personal Diary of Our World-wide Ministry.* Tulsa: Oral Roberts, 1968.
_____. *My Twenty Years of a Miracle Ministry.* Tulsa: Oral Roberts, 1956.
Rosenberg, Bernard, and David Manning White, eds. *Mass Culture.* New York: Crowell-Collier, 1957.

Schramm, Wilbur. *The Impact of Educational Television.* Urbana: University of Illinois, 1960.
_____. *Mass Communications.* Urbana: University of Illinois, 1960.
_____. *Mass Media and National Development.* Stanford: Stanford University, 1965.
Schramm, Wilbur; Lyle, Jack; and Edwin B. Parker. *Television in the Lives of Our Children.* Stanford: Stanford University, 1961.
Seipmann, C. A. *Radio and Television and Society.* New York: Oxford U. P., 1950.
Seldes, G. *The Great Audience.* New York: Viking, 1951.
Sellers, James E. *The Outsider and the Word of God.* New York: Abingdon, 1961.
Shayon, Robert Lewis, comp. *The Eighth Art.* New York: Holt, Rinehart and Winston, 1962.
Sheen, Fulton S. *Life Is Worth Living.* New York: McGraw, 1955.
Shinn, Roger L. *Tangled World.* New York: Scribner, 1965.
Siller, B.; White, I.; and H. Terkel. *Television and Radio News.* New York: Macmillan, 1960.

Skilbeck, Oswald. *ABC of Film and TV Working Terms.* New York: Hastings House, 1960.
Skornin, H. J.; Lee, Robert H.; and Fred A. Brewer. *Creative Broadcasting.* New York: Prentice-Hall, 1950.
Skornia, Harry. *Television and Society.* New York: McGraw-Hill, 1965.
Smith, M. H., ed. *Using Television for the Classroom.* New York: McGraw-Hill, 1961.
Southern Baptist Radio and Television Commission. *1969-1970 Commission Handbook.* Fort Worth: International Communications Center, 1969.
Stein, Barney. *Spot News Photography.* New York: Amphoto, 1960.
Steinberg, Charles S. *Mass Media and Communication.* New York: Hastings House, 1965.
Steiner, Gary A. *The People Look at Television.* New York: Knopf, 1963.
Stowe, Everett M. *Communicating Reality Through Symbols.* Philadelphia: Westminster (Westminster Studies in Christian Communication Series), 1966.
Stumpers, Frans Louis Henri Marie. *A Bibliography of Information Theory, Communication Theory—Cybernetics.* Cambridge, Mass.: M.I.T., 1953.
Summers, R. E., and H. B. Summers. *Broadcasting and the Public.* Belmont, Cal.: Wadsworth, 1966.
Swallow, M. *Factual Television.* New York: Hastings House, 1966.

Taylor, Marvin J. *Religious and Moral Education.* New York: The Center for Applied Research in Education, 1965.
Taylor, S. W., ed. *Radio Programming in Action.* New York: Hastings House, 1967.
Thelen, Herbert A. *Education and the Human Quest.* New York: Harper and Brothers, 1960.
Tillich, Paul. *Theology of Culture.* New York: Oxford U. P., 1964.
Trueblood, Elton. *The Company of the Committed.* New York: Harper and Row, 1961.

United States Federal Communications Commission. *Public Service Responsibility of Broadcast Licensees.* Washington, D.C.: Federal Communications Commission, 1946.
_____. *Report on Chain Broadcasting.* Washington, D.C.: United States Government Printing Office, 1941.

Vivas, Eliseo, and Murray Krieger. *The Problems of Aesthetics.* New York: Holt, Rinehart and Winston, 1953.

Wainwright, Charles Anthony. *The Television Copywriter: How To Create Successful TV Commercials.* New York: Hastings House, 1963.

MODELS OF RELIGIOUS BROADCASTING

Ward, L. B. *Father Charles E. Coughlin.* Detroit: Tower Publications, 1933.
Warshow, Robert. *The Immediate Experience.* New York: Anchor, 1962.
Wedel, Theodore O. *The Gospel in a Strange New World.* Philadelphia: Westminster (Westminster Studies in Christian Communication Series), 1963.
Wilette, Leo, and Jim Atkins, Jr. *Filming TV News and Documentaries.* New York: Amphoto, 1965.
Willis, E. E. *Writing Television and Radio Programs.* New York: Holt, Rinehart and Winston, 1966.
Wilson, Edmund. *Classics and Commercials.* New York: Farrar, Strauss and Giroux, 1950.
Wittich, Walter, and Charles Schuller. *Audio Visual Materials, Their Nature and Use.* New York: Harper and Brothers, 1962.
Wood, William A. *Electric Journalism.* New York and London: Columbia University, 1967.
Woolbert, Charles M. *The Fundamentals of Speech.* New York: Harper, 1920.
Wright, Charles R. *Mass Communication, A Sociological Perspective.* New York: Random House, 1959.

Zettl, Herbert. *Television Production Handbook.* San Francisco: Wadsworth, 1961.
_____. *Television Production Workbook.* San Francisco: Wadsworth, 1964.

Journals, Periodicals and Unpublished Papers

Aikman, Duncan. "Savanarola in Los Angeles," *American Mercury,* Vol. XI, No. 84.
Amplify, Vol. III, No. 4; Vol. IV, Nos. 1 and 6; Vol. V, Nos. 3 and 6; Vol. VI, Nos. 1, 2, 3, 5, and 6; Vol. VII, Nos. 1 and 2; Vol. VIII, Nos. 1 and 5; Vol. IX, Nos. 1, 4, 5, and 6; Vol. X, Nos. 2 and 5; Vol. XII, No. 6.
Aske, Sigurd. "What Makes a Radio Programme Christian?" *The Christian Broadcaster,* Vol. XV, No. 1.

Comstock, Sarah. "Aimee Semple McPherson—Prima Donna of Revivalism," *Harper's Magazine,* Dec. 1927.
"Come Blow Your Horn." TRAV Promotional.
Coon, Roger W. "The Public Speaking of Dr. William A. Fagal of 'Faith for Today,' America's First National Television Pastor." Unpublished dissertation, Michigan State University, 1970.
"Council on Mass Media Report of Program Committee Activities of the Division of Mass Media to the Standing Committee on Mass Media, 182nd General Assembly." Unpublished document of the

BIBLIOGRAPHY

Division of Mass Media of the United Presbyterian Church in the United States of America.

Cox, Harvey. "Is TV Seducing Our Souls?", *The Sunday News Magazine of The Detroit News*, Sept. 23, 1973.

Cox, Kenneth A. "The FCC, The Churches, and Public Responsibility in Broadcasting." Unpublished document. West Palm Beach, Fla.: National Conference of Christian Broadcasters, 1968.

Crowe, Charles M. "Religion on the Air," *The Christian Century*, IX (Aug. 23, 1944).

Doan, Richard K. "That Old Time Religion Brought Up To Date," *TV Guide*, Dec. 20, 1969.

Douglas, Robert. "How TV's Top Preacher Built a $14 Million Empire," *Toronto Daily Star*, May 1, 1971.

Duncan, Ray. "Fighting Bob Shuler—the Holy Terror," *Los Angeles Magazine*, Vol. VIII, No. 3.

Eastman, Fred. "Religion and the Radio," *The Christian Century*, LVIII (March 6, 1941).

Eesinoun, Bernard. "Reflections of a Radio Priest," *Focus Midwest*, Feb. 1963.

Ellens, J. Harold. "The Back to God Hour Radio Broadcasting." Unpublished document, Wayne State University, 1968.

———. "The Order of the Franciscans, A Study in Mission." Unpublished occasional paper, 1972.

Federal Council Bulletin, VII (Nov./Dec. 1924); XIV (April 1932).

Finnigan, Joseph. "The Spiritual Soft Sell of Father Emery Tang," *TV Guide*, March 18, 1972.

Fore, William F. "A Short History of Religious Broadcasting." Unpublished document prepared for the National Council of Churches of Christ Broadcasting and Film Commission, 1967.

Four Square, May 1954, Dec. 1923, and Sept. 1924.

Gockel, Herman W. "Historical Material on *This Is the Life.*" Unpublished document, St. Louis, Mo., 1967.

———. "Some Basic Factors Governing the Church's Use of Mass Media." Unpublished document, St. Louis, Mo., undated.

Gunther, Max. "TV and the New Morality," *TV Guide*, Oct. 14, 1972.

Johnson, Nicholas. "The Careening of America," *The Humanist*, July/Aug. 1972.

Journal of Broadcasting, Vol. IX, No. 2; Vol. X, No. 2; Vol. XIII, No. 1.

Lutheran Television Productions. *Christmas Is.* Marketing flier.

Mack, S. Franklin. "Cooperation in the Use of the Media of Mass

Communication." Unpublished occasional paper, Office of Communication, United Church of Christ, 1970.

McPherson, Aimee Semple. "On My Fortieth Anniversary, A Brief History of the Foursquare Gospel." Unpublished, undated pamphlet.

Milton, G. Ralph. "The Church and the Media—A Summary of Some Relevant Research." Unpublished document. Undated.

Parker, Everett C. "Christian Communication and Secular Man." Unpublished document, Office of Communication, United Church of Christ, undated.

"Preaching to a Nation," *Review of Reviews*, LXXIX (Feb. 1929).

Price, Nelson. "Media: Key to Development." New York: TRAFCO, undated.

———. "Memo to Harry C. Spenser." Unpublished document, New York, undated.

———. "Working Policy and Practice for Radio and Television Programming: Methodist Church." Unpublished document, New York, 1966.

Robinson, Haddon. "An Analysis of Attitudes Toward Religious Radio and Television Programs." Unpublished document of the Division of Radio and Television of the United Presbyterian Church of the United States of America, 1962.

Rodgers, W. W. "Broadcasting Church Services," *Radio Broadcast*, Vol. I (Aug. 1922).

Rogers, Howard E. "The Churches and the Mass Media," *Messenger*, March 27, 1969.

Smedes, Lewis B. "Prudery and Pornography," *The Reformed Journal*, Sept. 1973.

SBC-RTC. "Network Television Exposures," "A Series of 16 Documentaries," and "A Series of 26 Documentaries." Promotional sheets.

SBC-RTC. "Romans by Saint Paul," Feb. 1, 1968.

SBC-RTC. News releases, Dec. 11, 1969; June 8, 1970.

SBC-RTC. *The Human Dimension*. Programming marketing bulletin.

SBC-RTC. "A World Within Our Reach." Promotional brochure.

SBC-RTC. "Programming Marketing Bulletin," for JOT.

"Some Problems in the Broadcasting of Religion," *Radio Broadcast*, IV (Nov. 1923).

"Some Questions and Answers About Southern Baptist Radio-TV Commission." RTC promotional brochure.

Spargur, Ronn. "Can Churches Break the Prime-Time Barrier?", *Christianity Today*, Jan. 16, 1970.

"Stringent Code Is Submitted to Industry," *Broadcasting*, XVI (June 15, 1939).

BIBLIOGRAPHY

"Tangled World: New Television Series for Thinking Adults." WCC promotional pamphlet.

Telenotes, May 1955 and May 1965.

Terry, Clifford. "It's a Far Cry from the Church in the Wildwood," *TV Guide*, Sept. 12, 1972.

Van den Heuvel, Albert. "Broadcaster: Priest and Prophet." Unpublished address at WACC-NABS. Florida, Nov. 1971.

Index

Alexander, John, 21, 97-100
Allen, Steve, 131
American Broadcasting Company (ABC), 18, 31
American Council of Churches, 20, 33
Angell, James Roland, 29
Angelus Temple, 71-74
Archbishop of Canterbury, 111, 136
Armstrong, Garner Ted, 64-65
Armstrong, Herbert W., 61, 64-65

Baldwin, Edward, 138
Beemer, Brace, 45
Bell, Alexander Graham, 13
Bell, L. Nelson, 98
"Biblical Perspectives," 99

Boone, Pat, 87
Boyd, Bernard, 99
Boyles, N. S., 98
Brackbill, Charles, 126, 128-131
Broadcasting and Film Commission of the National Council of Churches, 19-20, 127-128, 140
Bryant, Anita, 87

Cadman, S. Parkes, 17, 27, 64
Carino, Lawrence, 147
Carmichael, Ralph, 87
Carothers, George, 137
Carson, Johnny, 136
Cathedral of Tomorrow, 74-78
Cavett, Dick, 136
Christian Reformed Church, 36, 46-55, 144

INDEX

Columbia Broadcasting System (CBS), 18, 31, 33, 44, 56, 137, 147
"Come Blow Your Horn," 99-100, 134
Cooley, Denton, 106
Coon, Roger W., 113
Coughlin, Charles E., 19, 29, 55-61, 65
Cox, Harvey, 149-151

DeBakey, Michael, 106
Decision, 91
DeHaan, M. R., 29, 64, 97
DeHaan, Richard, 97
Department of National Religious Radio of the Federal Council of Churches of Christ, 17
Detroit Council of Churches, 138
"Dialogue," 138
"Directions," 105
Division of Radio and Television of the Protestant Episcopal Church, 123
Dodd, Bobby, 98
Douglas, Mike, 131
Dumaurier, George, 14
Durante, Jimmy, 87

Educational Television Program Services, 100
Eldersveld, Peter, 29, 47-50, 54, 61, 65
Elliott, W., Jr., 98
Evans, Dale, 87

Fagal, William A., 109-114
"Faith for Today," 109-114
Federal Communications Commission (FCC), 15, 29, 142-144, 145, 150
Federal Council of Churches of Christ (FCCC), 17-25, 27-32, 33-34, 140
Federal Radio Commission, 29, 63, 143
Fessenden, Reginald Aubrey, 14
Fosdick, Harry Emerson, 27, 64

Franciscan Order, 130-133
Freberg, Stan, 128
"Frontiers of Faith," 105
Frost, David, 136
Fuller, Charles E., 29, 61, 64, 65

Gilbert, Richard, 126, 131
Glide, Lizzie, 62
Gockel, Herman W., 115-119
"Good Ship Grace," 64
Goodman, Frank C., 17, 27
Gordon, Lou, 137
Gortner, Marjoe, 91
Graham, Billy, 69, 70, 88-91, 91, 93
Graham, Virginia, 131
Gunther, Max, 145-146

Hamblin, Stuart, 89
Hammond, Kirk, 134
Harding, Warren G., 16
Harrington, Bob, 65
Hertz, Heinrich, 14
Hestir, Bluford B., 99, 133-134
Hoffmann, Oswald C. J., 44-46, 61, 65
"Hour of Decision," 90-91, 92
How to Talk Back to Your Television Set, 150
Humbard, Maude Aimee Jones (Mrs. Rex), 75, 77-78
Humbard, Rex, 69, 70, 74-80, 85, 90, 91, 93
Humbard, Rex, Jr., 77-78
Hutton, David, 71

Jennings, Ralph M., 23
Johnson, Nicholas, 150-151
Joint Religious Radio Commission (JRRC), 19, 23, 31, 32-33, 36, 140
Jolly, Russell, 129
Jones, Wayne, 78
"Jot," 106-107

Kennedy, Dana, 124
Kennedy, John F., 16
Kernochan, Howard, 91
Kernochan, Sarah, 91
Knudsen, Walther S., 45
Kuhns, William, 35

INDEX

"Lamp Unto My Feet," 105, 137
"Layman's Witness," 98
Leo XIII, Pope, 59
"Let's See," 138
Lewis, Jerry, 87
Libby, Robert, 124, 135
"Life Is Worth Living," 42
Lutheran Church in America, 22
Lutheran Church—Missouri Synod, 21, 24, 44-46, 113, 114-122, 127
Lutheran Layman's League, 115
Lutheran Television Productions, 117-121, 132

McDaniel, Don, 99
MacFarland, Charles S., 28
McGlohon, Loonis, 100
McMaster, Larry, 138
McPherson, Aimee Semple, 29, 61, 70-74, 91, 93, 97
McPherson, Harold, 71
Mack, Franklin, 23
Maier, Walter, 21, 24, 44-45, 61, 65, 89, 115
"Man to Man," 98
Marjoe, 91
Marty, Martin E., 142, 145, 147-149
"Mayflower Doctrine," 15, 143
Methodist Radio and Film Commission, 22
Meyers, Bob, 64
Muggeridge, Malcolm, 105, 137
Mutual Broadcasting System, 18, 31, 33, 45, 47, 50, 74
"My Answer," 91

National Association of Broadcasters, 29
National Association of Evangelicals, 20, 32, 33
National Board of Catholic Bishops, 138
National Broadcasting Company (NBC), 17, 18, 30-33, 47, 50
National Council of Catholic Men, 33
National Council of Churches of Christ in the USA (NCC), 19-20, 36, 99, 105, 144
"National Radio Pulpit," 17, 27, 64, 65
National Religious Advisory Council of NBC, 17
National Vocations Office, 138
Nederhood, Joel, 36, 50-54, 61, 65
Neeb, Martin J., Jr., 61, 119-122, 127, 132

O'Brien, Morgan J., 28
"Old Fashioned Revival Hour," 64
Oral Roberts University, 84

Parker, Everett C., 19, 22, 24, 28, 32-37, 100-102, 136, 140-145, 148, 152
Pastore, John, 145
Pius XII, Pope, 40
Presbyterian Church US, 21, 97-100
Protestant Episcopal Church, 21, 123-126
Protestant Radio and TV Center, 98
Protestant Radio Commission of FCCC, 19, 22, 24
"Puntito," 107
"Put God First," 98

Radio Act of 1912, 15, 143
Radio Act of 1927, 15, 143
Radio Act of 1934, 15, 143
Radio and TV Commission for the Southern Baptist Convention, 102-109
"Radio Bible Class," 64, 97
Raiford, Bob, 100
Rakestraw, Caroline, 123
Read, David H. C., 27, 64
Redhead, J. A., 98
Rerum Novarum 59
Reston, James, 34
Roberts, Oral, 69, 70, 80-88, 90, 91, 93
Roberts, Richard, 87
Rogers, Jimmy, 87

INDEX

Roosevelt, Franklin D., 16, 55, 57
Rosenwald, Julius, 28
Ross, Dick, 87

Sarnoff, David, 15
Semple, Robert, 70
Seventh Day Adventist Church, 109-114
Shaw, Marlena, 100
Sheen, Fulton J., 29, 38-44, 59, 65
Shinn, Roger L., 97, 100-101, 141
Shuler, Robert Pierce, 61-63, 65
Social Justice, 57, 58
Sockman, Ralph, 27, 64
Southern Baptist Convention, 21, 23-24, 102-109, 127
Southern Religious Radio Conference (SRRC), 20-23, 98, 103
Spargur, Ronn, 34
Spellman, Francis Cardinal, 40-41
Stevens, Paul, 36, 54, 102-109, 127, 135, 137
Stout, David, 137
Susskind, David, 137

Taft, William Howard, 14
Tang, Emery, 130-133
"Tangled World," 100-101, 141
"Telespots," 131
"The Answer," 79, 106, 107
"The Back to God Hour," 36, 46-55
"The Bible Auditorium of the Air," 110
"The Family Religious Telecast," 112
"The Human Dimension," 106, 107
"The Lutheran Hour," 21-22, 24, 44-46, 89, 115
"The Protestant Hour," 21
The Seduction of the Spirit, 149
"This Is the Answer," 104
"This Is the Life," 24, 113, 114-120
Thomson, Robert, 129
"Thought for the Day," 124
"Today," 136
TRAV, 98-100, 133-134
Turner, Patsy, 98

United Church of Christ, 22, 100-102, 140-145
United Church of Christ Office of Communication, 100, 140
United Methodist Church, 22, 136
United Presbyterian Church in the USA, 20-21, 25, 99, 126-130, 136

Vaus, Jim, 89

Williams, Anne, 86
Wilson, Woodrow, 15

Young, Owen D., 15